David Gentleman's London

London from Primrose Hill

David Gentleman's London

Weidenfeld and Nicolson
London

for Sue

Copyright © David Gentleman 1985
First published in hardcover in Great Britain 1985
First published in paperback in Great Britain 1986
George Weidenfeld & Nicolson Limited
91 Clapham High Street
London sw4 7ta

All rights reserved. No part of this publication may
be reproduced, stored in a retrieval system, or
transmitted in any form or by any means, electronic,
mechanical, photocopying, recording or otherwise,
without the prior permission of the copyright owner.

isbn 0 297 78831 0

Colour separations by Newsele Litho Ltd
Filmset by Keyspools Ltd, Golborne, Lancashire
Printed in Italy by L.E.G.O., Vicenza

Contents

Introduction 6

The River 12

The Thames Barrier – Greenwich – London's dockland – Wapping and Bermondsey
Blackfriars and Cannon Street – Southwark and the City bank – King's Reach and St Paul's
County Hall and Westminster – Battersea and Hammersmith– Chiswick and Mortlake

The City and the East End 34

Prospects from the City – The Roman and medieval City – The Tower of London
Leadenhall Market and St Paul's – Wren's churches and the Monument
Ceremony in the City – The horizontal City – The vertical City – City detail – Holborn and Gough Square
The Law Courts and Middle Temple – Lincoln's Inn Fields – The new City and Bunhill Fields
Fournier Street and Spitalfields – The East End markets – The East End today

Westminster and St James's 68

Parliament and the Abbey – Dean's Yard and Smith Square – Horse Guards Parade
Embankment Gardens and the MoD – Queen Anne's Gate and the Mall
The Palace and Number Ten – St James's Palace – Trafalgar Square
Waterloo Place and Pall Mall – St James's Square

The Parks 90

St James's Park and Whitehall – Green Park and the Broad Walk
Hyde Park and Rotten Row – Hyde Park and Kensington Gardens – Regent's Park
The Canal and the Zoo – Primrose Hill – Parliament Hill Fields – Hampstead Heath
Victoria Park and Peckham Rye – Epping Forest and Richmond Park

The West End 114

Street traders – Soho – The British Museum and Gower Street – West End pubs
Theatres – Opera House and street theatre – Covent Garden: the Piazza
Tottenham Court Road and Fitzrovia – Euston Road – The railway stations
Langham Place and Camden Lock – Berkeley Square – Mayfair and Grosvenor Square
Park Lane – Hyde Park Corner – West End shops – Belgravia – South Kensington

Villages and Suburbs 152

Dulwich, Greenwich and Blackheath – Ham, Chiswick and Hampstead
Hurlingham and Putney – Church Row and Downshire Hill – The history of the terrace
Camden Town markets – Camden Town and Primrose Hill – Ladbroke Grove and Notting Hill
Chelsea and the King's Road – Hendon and Kew – The Regent's Canal
The railways and the underground – Terraces and semis – Turnpikes and motorways
Neasden, Paddington and Brixton – Brent Cross flyover – The Thames at Richmond

Index 191

Introduction

I came to London as a student and have stayed on for thirty-four years. My home and studio is in Camden Town, in the midst of a landscape whose contrasts and juxtapositions are themselves typical of London. Out of one window I can see a crescent of early-Victorian houses, many of them occupied by people who both live and work there, the gardens shaded by limes and plane trees. Over the rooftops are the Post Office Tower, the Dutch-Victorian gables of the primary school to which my children have gone, and the trees of Primrose Hill. The other window looks onto a grim but handsome Edwardian red-brick doss-house, a council depot, an empty thirties bread factory, a railway, council flats and a street of houses turned into shops. There is also a street market looking more like a fairground and a big cinema turned over to bingo, its recessed fire exits often occupied by men and women who shelter, get drunk, piss and sleep there. Away to the north the ground rises to the slopes of Parliament Hill Fields and the heights of Highgate, while to the south are the gothic spires of St Pancras and beyond these the Barbican and the other recent City tower blocks. But the foreground is the bit of London I know best, the only bit I really feel part of. With all its splendour and squalors the great city is a remarkable spectacle but not something which one can always identify with: the place is far too big for that. And yet, when its good things are destroyed or cheapened, I feel a sense of loss.

Even as a small boy brought up twenty miles away I had formed a clear picture of London. But it was not so much of the middle of London, which left only fragmented impressions of treats, the Zoo and the Science Museum and John Lewis's, my father's 'office' (a design studio high over the Thames) and the open-air theatre just before the war. The sharpest picture in my mind was of the train journey 'up', which was the best bit; and like many first impressions it is still pretty reliable. It fixed London once and for all as a place surrounded first by open countryside, then by leafy suburbia whose houses grew closer-set and older as the journey went on; they thickened at length into something my parents called 'slums' but which I now know consisted really of neat Victorian slate-roof terraces

with sooty walls but with fresh little gardens behind them. Each gas-lit railway station had the same enamelled ads for Virol, Bovril, Mazawattee and Stephens' Inks. Towards the end of the journey there were deserts of sidings with horsedrawn Charrington's coal-carts, tall brick chimneys with brand-names painted on them, and a soot-encrusted tunnel in which the train invariably stopped until finally one emerged among the gasometers, arches and vaults of King's Cross.

Later, as a student in the early fifties, I filled in more of the inner London details: South Kensington and Battersea, the parks and the river with its rusting lighters clanking and booming as the tide banged them together. But that London would seem unfamiliar now. Reconstruction after the war had hardly begun, and it was quite an event to see a new building, for London was still largely a Victorian city, still blacked out even then by the last of the choking Dickensian fogs. Now, the railway soot has gone, and the fog with it; King's Cross and St Pancras are brick-coloured again, not black. But car smog, traffic noise and concrete fill the sky in their place; the rusty lighters on the river mud now serve as landing pads for helicopters.

One of my early jobs was drawing for a Sunday newspaper a series of imaginary impressions of the new London that was then just about to take over; how the new Hilton and the Hyde Park Corner underpass would look, what it might be like if Leicester Square were pedestrianized, how the London Wall tower blocks and the Shell building would look when they were finished. For better or for worse these things all happened, and the bits of London they replaced now seem part of history, as distant and forgotten as open buses, trams and horse-cabs.

What I know of London's earlier history has also been learnt through my work, drawing the bits of it that are still standing around or have since disappeared. Through drawing it I realized that the Roman Wall by the Tower for instance is more than just a thrown-together pile of ragstone, flint and tile: its solidity is a reminder that Roman London was already important enough strategic-ally to *need* walling-in against marauders. It was not an administrative centre but simply the first place where a firm gravel bluff made it possible to cross the Thames by a ford, ferry or bridge. Later on, the Normans established their court and church some distance upstream at Westminster; they could have sacked the city; realizing its usefulness, they left it alone. But they built the Tower as a stern token of their might just outside the city limits.

In medieval times, the wall was more elaborately fortified. It completely enclosed the town to landward: its bastions can be seen along London Wall and near the Tower. The city owes its ground-plan to being squashed within this medieval wall, and many alleys and narrow streets still bear witness to it, though their wooden houses were all burnt down in the Great Fire of 1666. The higgledy-piggledy ground-plan survived because, though Wren and John Evelyn and others suggested more ambitious and formal re-arrangements with the avenues, vistas, *ronds-points*, squares and circuses already familiar in France and Italy, no one could impose them on a city parcelled out between many private individuals. All that could be agreed was to build two new thoroughfares with the appropriately grand names of Queen Street and King Street to link the Guildhall better with the river. But what Wren *did* leave behind was a great cathedral in an idiom novel to London, whose fine dome became a symbol of the City and indeed of the capital; and a wonderful series of churches with towers and spires thrown off with masterly abandon. This happy result of a haphazard set of circumstances is itself a national feature: Britain has never then or since had the kind of authoritarian regime that would make steam-roller Haussmann-style planning possible, nor, if it comes to that, a monarchy strong enough even to build itself from scratch a proper London palace. So all that remains now to remind us of the opportunities for orderly restoration lost after the Fire are St Paul's and those of Wren's City churches that may still be glimpsed now and then between the office blocks. Yet there was another positive if less obvious result. The restrained, even austere eighteenth-century brick façades which we associate with the West End owe their appearance to building regulations intended to prevent any more Great Fires.

In the seventeenth and eighteenth centuries, London spread in large chunks northwards from the palaces along the river bank or strand. The great landowners like the Bedfords, the Grosvenors and the Cavendishes saw that orderly, planned development would attract grander leaseholders and thus keep up the long-term value of their properties better than haphazard piecemeal growth for quicker profit. For this reason, their designs – Inigo Jones's for Covent Garden, Lord St Albans' for St James's Square and Leverton's for Bedford Square – included not only fine squares and terraces of houses, but mews and stables, churches and markets also. They thus provided for all needs, including those of the useful lower orders as well as the grander ones, helping to create that social mixture

which used to be one of London's more noticeable features. And the houses they built had many uses, for most of the city's professional, commercial and even industrial activities went on behind their rational, adaptable and modest brick façades. Churches and barracks were built for specific requirements, but apart from the big warehouses, very few eighteenth-century commercial structures in London were purpose-built.

Eastcheap

By the nineteenth century however, industrialism required custom-built factories, offices and institutions like proper banks and big new markets. It also saw the arrival of the railways. These last created two important new features: the blighted wedges between the main railway lines turned into slums and, when cheap workmen's tickets made it possible for the first time for a working man to live away from his job, new single-class suburbs grew up among the remoter villages. Since Victorian industrialism was far too new and overwhelming to control, it is not surprising that its effect on London was on a monumental scale. Yet even a minor local change might have wider repercussions: the removal in 1837 of the monarchy from St James's to Buckingham Palace was enough to trigger off the transformation of the nearby market gardens of newly smart Belgravia into the splendid terraces and squares we see today.

But if such buildings suggest a growing prosperity, the public buildings of the age of Victoria reflect its growing unreality. The pseudo-renaissance style of Palmerston's Foreign Office and the pseudo-medievalism of the Natural History Museum and even of Westminster itself, beautiful as they all are, suggest a newly uncertain and unself-confident age, buoying itself up with nostalgic medievalism and later with the heady rhetorical trappings of imperial pomp just when it felt its competitive industrial edge beginning to wear down as others caught up. The aspects of London that most truthfully reflect the realities of the nineteenth century are not the great imperial monuments but the terraces of housing for the lower and middle classes.

Late-Victorian and Edwardian imperialism spawned yet more overblown government and commercial offices, and also incidentally the lovely *Boy's Own Paper* statuary of Whitehall and St James's. But the buildings were left behind by developments elsewhere that even the better

English architects were too prosperous, too stuffy and too insular to notice. They were basically unaware of or antipathetic to modernism: even by 1939 London had chalked up only a handful of buildings imaginatively and candidly using twentieth-century techniques for their own sakes. This meant that when, after the relatively minor effects of the blitz and the pause caused by post-war austerity, local authorities and developers got together to knock down and rebuild enormous expanses of London, there was at first no native tradition of understanding and experience to apply to the new materials and industrial techniques of present-day architecture. The more durable results of this dismal period will be left standing around London for a long time. But not *all* the new buildings are ugly or shoddy. Much local-authority housing is good and imaginative; office-building in the City has got better as architects have grown cleverer. The plum jobs, however, generally go not to the best but to the wiliest.

In making this book, I have adopted a general arrangement by area. It starts with the river, London's *raison d'être*, the ancient highway into the city, and still the best place from which to stand back and take a look at it; it looks next at the City and the areas on its doorstep; and it moves upstream to the other ancient centres of Westminster, Whitehall and St James's. It then retreats for relaxation into the parks and open spaces; explores the West End; and finally looks at the surrounding areas and at London's perpetual and irresistible expansion outwards. But these are not completely clear-cut or precise divisions; indeed, it is impossible to chop up London into such hard and fast segments. One has to get out a map to find exactly where, say, the City ends – one does not feel it by instinct, in the way in which a resident can sense where Camden Town turns into Kentish Town or Chalk Farm. Indeed, most people who live in London know their immediate surroundings, the schools, shops, markets, tube stations and so on, very intimately; but they visit the rest of London, even the places they work in, almost as strangers.

But there is one boundary real enough in many senses. London is cut in two by the river: more so than can be explained merely by the physical barrier. There have been many attempts to draw south and north London closer together: new road bridges like Southwark, Blackfriars and Westminster in the eighteenth and nineteenth centuries, railway bridges in the nineteenth, and the careful siting of County Hall, the Festival of Britain and the theatres, cinemas, concert-halls and galleries on the South Bank today. Yet the two shores stubbornly remain as far apart as they were in Shakespeare's time, when to get to a theatre at all you had to leave the city altogether and cross the river. Smart London has in any case tended to spread north and above all west; one can still live just south of the river more cheaply than is possible in the north or west, even in areas like Camden Town, Islington and Notting Hill which

used themselves to be thought remote and shabby. This renewal and re-invigoration, though unhappily it often gets done at the expense of the people who previously lived there, regenerates areas that have become tacky and run-down, adding to the changes of key that make London so interesting to look at.

These contrasts are not just architectural and social. London offers not only the interest of fine buildings and (equally important) the way they have been grouped, but also the wide perspectives of river and parks, the inexhaustibly fascinating spectacle of people at work, and the curiosity of the details – a bronze water-nymph or a battered tramp, a fruit-barrow or a cast-iron park bench, a pub mirror or a parking-meter. Some of its 'sights' are essentially three-dimensional experiences: the arches and passageways of the Tower, the lofty spaciousness of the Abbey, the dream-like oddity of Sir John Soane's Museum, the clever organization, in St Paul's and the National Theatre, of their space and our movement. Other spectacles are to be experienced as if one were wandering about a stage set: brick-and-mortar for a history play at St James's Palace, stone at Bunhill Fields, leafy stucco in Keats Grove, Hampstead. Other buildings again such as Kent's Horse Guards for instance, or Kenwood, are primarily to be enjoyed as flat backdrops. Very occasionally the pleasure is that of a grand formal conception, as with Wren's greatest bit of organization, the Royal Naval Hospital at Greenwich; but more often the delight is in the isolated gem-like detail, like the Wren City churches which one enjoys by mentally masking out their surroundings. And sometimes, as in the West End's fine squares, the pleasure comes from the way the parts – terraces, railings, trees and lawn – are all subordinated to the end of making a practical and agreeable whole. No other city can equal London for its squares and terraces, forms so handsome and satisfying that they go on looking good even when they are old and shabby.

Bedford Square

London's lesser delights are no less vivid, even if they are sometimes harder to find. The suburban gardens and allotments; the fresh green street markets; the delicate Georgian detail of the Spitalfields terraces; fragrant parks and canal banks, blossomy arterial roads and the leafy streets of Camden Town; all are a minor but delightful part of the city as a whole. Even such small things as iron balconies and railings, gleaming white window-surrounds, York-stone pavements, kerbside setts and prettily designed cast-iron coal hole covers and lamp-standards, all contribute to the satisfying overall beauty of a London street, well-knit and unified because it was built all in one go. But such unity is easily broken by a false note, a change of key; and more and more London scenes look striking for the very opposite reason, because of a dramatic contrast, a sharp change of mood, usually architectural. St Paul's framed by Cannon Street Station is an instance from the past, the Barbican encasing St Bride's and the relation of the Tower to the NatWest Tower are recent ones. The newest of all is the razed-flat East End seen between the shiny brand-new cowls of the Flood Barrier.

St Mary Somerset

Weather and light often make these contrasts more dramatic still. I have seen the City skyline late on a very hot afternoon when a dark sky promised thunder and all the colour had drained away out of St Paul's, and the tall office blocks turned into a sort of white flare; the buildings looked so hot they might catch light. Some effects depend on motion that you cannot draw: stray shafts of sunlight moving across a London landscape briefly light up white buildings as though a switch is being turned on and off.

But these sights, new and startling as they are, are common to all tall new cities: you see better skyscrapers in New York, and a lot more of them. And of the famous sights that are unique to London, some of the most conspicuous are disappointing and even shaming let-downs. Leicester Square is a squalid and commercialized mess, Piccadilly Circus a mere set-down point for Culture Buses between a neon poster cliff, some amusement arcades, and a few tatty old theatres. They don't *look* nice. They're famous only for being famous; whereas much that is best in London catches you by surprise when you're not looking. Crossing St James's Park to its tube station for instance, you suddenly find yourself on a footbridge with an astonishing view over a willowy lake towards a distant

Whitehall skyline of magical domes and spires; a couple of minutes later you are looking into the most perfect 1700s street in existence, Queen Anne's Gate. And some of London's best things have to be searched for. Dean's Yard at Westminster, Lincoln's Inn and the Inns of Court have to be entered through private-looking gateways; the fantastic industrial canyon of Shad Thames is obscurely hidden away even though it is only just across Tower Bridge, yet it offers just as vivid a picture of what London was really like as the Tower itself. If one can take the time to explore, and look closely enough, London's pleasures are inexhaustible.

But many of London's delights, however intense, are all too fragile. London is like a stately home where the current caretakers, cramped for space and feeling that things have got shabby, have thrown out the antique furniture and covered the garden with asphalt to make room for parking. London has been quite powerless to keep the car at bay. In the inner city it now furs up the arteries, throttling public transport and wasting far more human energy than it saves; and in the suburbs it either slices through with speedways so lethal that people have to be fenced off like cattle, or else it takes to the air, sailing over the sea of roof-tops and blotting out the sky with concrete. What is more, traffic is indiscriminate: places as grand as Apsley House and Park Lane have fallen victim to its effects just as pathetically as humbler suburban houses. And just when traffic roaring on the flyover and parked on the doorstep has come to seem permanent, buildings have begun to seem temporary. On London's skyline, the old ornamental spikes of church spires and belfries, chimneys and towers have been overlaid by utilitarian vertical slabs for people to live or work in. Some of these slabs are elegant and beautiful, but many are ugly and shoddily constructed. Yet in building them, the councils and their architects laid waste much serviceable, good-looking and restorable building, and replaced it with expensive, short-lived and conspicuous makeshifts. Many of these, like Taylor Woodrow's ill-starred Ronan Point, made money for contractors and architects. The occupants were the sufferers and the authorities were left with un-paid-off and unmaintainable white elephants. And even if fashions have changed and the newer toy-town housing estates are low and brick-coloured again, it is the tall blocks which will be there for a long time as reminders.

Dismayed by this spectacle, it is tempting to search for a culprit and easiest to blame the architects. But this is naive. Certainly, as theorists and even gurus, some architects helped to create the climate for the tower blocks. But though architecture has been called frozen music, most architects only play the notes: they don't call the tune. Local authorities and the developers are equally involved; and even they are not really to blame. The councils were doing their best honestly to improve the lot of their people. And even the richest developers were only cashing in on circumstances; they didn't create them. London simply hasn't known how to rebuild itself, how to cope; its buildings are the side effects, the symptoms of something wrong, not the cause. Technology and politics both play a part in this. As new building methods have developed, buildings have not merely proliferated: they have stopped seeming permanent and have started to look as impermanent as the prefabs of the forties; some of them almost as temporary as cars themselves. And under changing political pressures the town planners seem to have given up as hopeless the duty of acting as referees in a free economy, becoming instead the developers' allies – gamekeepers turned poachers. The effect of these changes is that London no longer adequately replaces the good things it destroys. What we are building here now will hardly tempt anyone to visit the place in the future. The Covent Garden piazza, Inigo Jones's Banqueting Hall, even St Paul's may be interesting in themselves, but their new surroundings are no great shakes. Most of the buildings are pretty faceless. Livelier ones like the TV-am studios are not serious architecture anyway but merely frozen jingles for an ad-financed industry whose output is all of a piece with the junk on the hoardings, the dogshit on the park grass and the lead in the air. The oldest-looking things, like the hopefully-named Dickens Inn at St Katharine's Dock and the pixie port next door, have been run up to impress the tourists only yesterday. For while the people who used to live there are forced out and the pretty corner-shops, the cheaper cafés and the more vulnerable small businesses go bust, London is being turned with calculated determination into a circus for visitors and natives alike.

But tighter money is slowing down the destruction. Nice buildings once again get left as they are because, as in Dublin, there is less money available to replace or ruin them. We are also learning to value them more intelligently; and, unless perhaps we are developers, to look more coldly at what might replace them. If we have less money to keep things up, we also have less inclination to mess them up.

In the meantime, however, London's traditionally relaxed and restrained style has changed. The city feels harsher and more dangerous than it did, with its barriers and its security checks, its speeding police cars and its periodic bombs. And as its minor amenities disappear, it gets more and more inconvenient: street name-plates vanish, public lavatories are closed, telephones do not work, and the dirty pavements are thick with barriers, meters and signs; and, adding insult to injury, shoddy sponsored litter-bins enjoin us, of all things, to Keep London Tidy. This last is more than a trivial irritant for it implies a new assumption: that tidiness – hitherto provided by the community – now needs a sponsor, and that the pavements too are now for sale.

Yet for all its drawbacks, London is still a good place to live in. If it is changing from a city of businesslike but discreet activity into an arena for self-conscious and if possible profitable happenings, it can't be helped; the same thing is taking place wherever big cities have lost their old roles and can't settle on new ones. In any case, it would be silly to dwell on what London used to be, or might have been: it can only be enjoyed for what it is; and much of that, if one keeps one's eyes open, is very beautiful. London is also a good place to work in, and there is a lot to see, enjoy, and use too: not just the written-about things like theatres and cinemas, galleries and museums, but also the libraries, schools and shops; even the street markets have better fruit and vegetables than you can buy anywhere else. But there is more to the city than stimulus and convenience. London is full of its past; in this country, it is the place where history has left the deepest and most visible traces, and where it is happening still, with implications often out of proportion to the small size of the country.

This mingling of past and present is always dramatically reflected in the London skyline. From Primrose Hill, on a mid-winter morning, the sun rises directly over the City. The red flush spreads up into the dark sky, revealing the toothed silhouettes of the Barbican flats and the NatWest Tower like milestones and bollards. In the half-light one begins to see that, though the scale has changed, the city skyline is still made up as it was in the eighteenth or indeed the sixteenth century of a few vertical accents rising above a level sea of lesser stuff. Then only moments later the strengthening morning light shows this enigmatic sea for what it really is: the same half-intended, half-accidental jumble of buildings, greenery, vehicles and people of which London has always consisted. Such effects of light pass quickly, like the changes in the face of London itself; but now and then they are striking enough to provoke one, as drawing also does, to notice the scene more intensely and, in doing so, to fix it in one's memory.

Camden Town 1984

The River

Without the Thames there would be no London. The Roman city owed its existence to the conjunction of tidal water to accommodate a fleet with a safe gravelly crossing-place where a bridge could be built. Later, in the Middle Ages, the river became the highway into London and the Tower its guardian, and by Tudor times, when Henry VIII established a dockyard at Deptford near his favourite palace of Greenwich, it was also its grand processional route and growing into Britain's most important port. From then on the river traffic, of poled barges and lighters and sailing ships, seen so vividly in the early prints of London, increased until by the early nineteenth century the banks were lined by rows of warehouses, wharves and tall cranes. Behind the banks on both sides of the river, east London gleamed with rectangles of unruffled dockland water, its big roads winding between the great docks' containing walls, its little streets already the first of the city's great overcrowded slums.

I used to enjoy drawing the lighters, the cranes, the warehouses and the bollarded Thames Street *culs-de-sac*, which ended in a flood wall and an iron ladder down to the mud and shingle of the foreshore. These things seemed there to stay. The most poignant bits of the riverside scene for me today are still the relics of all this activity; for relics are all that is now left. In the last few years, all the big ships and many of the others have vanished downstream to Tilbury and beyond, the river traffic being reduced in the main to oil barges, refuse lighters, police boats and excursion launches. It is an odd assortment to be passing through the spectacular Thames Barrier at Woolwich, the newest and strangest sight on the river.

London's splendours and headaches, her changed and changing nature are still dramatically visible from a trip on one of these launches, though it is not always easy to tell the extent of the change: the cranes may have gone and new office blocks taken their place, but the remaining riverside warehouses still look real enough from the water, even if they have in fact been gentrified into smart flats or artists' studios. But it is easy to realize from the razed-flat desolation that has replaced the Surrey Docks, or from the rows of multi-storey car-parks and the brand-new Dickensian riverside taverns on the City bank, that things have indeed altered. And where the relics of London's dockland still stand dramatic and empty but virtually unchanged as they do along Shad Thames, one knows this can only be a temporary respite in an inevitable process. Whether pulled down or tidied up, they will not last long: since I drew it, part of Shad Thames has already gone.

The best-looking view of the City and river nowadays is where one can see the new City skyline across King's Reach and over the South Bank foliage: if Wordsworth were writing the sonnet today, it would be 'Upon Waterloo Bridge'. Westminster has changed from a visual spectacle to a political one. Here, London's great seats of power – County Hall and Shell on the south bank, the Houses of Parliament on the north – eye one another across a divide both real and powerfully symbolic. Further upstream, the river becomes more industrial towards Battersea, and then, beyond Hammersmith, begins to turn rural again with poplars and willows, breweries and maltings, dinghies and houseboats to persuade one that urban London has been left behind.

Blackfriars and Southwark

The Thames Barrier under construction

Greenwich

Only a mile or two upstream from the remarkable Thames Barrier is London's most spectacular architectural conception, the Royal Naval Hospital at Greenwich. In 1616 Inigo Jones began building the Queen's House (in the middle), an Italian villa that must have seemed like a restrained classical box, for James I's Anne of Denmark; Jones's son-in-law John Webb added the river wing at the right of the picture in 1664; Wren had meanwhile suggested the conspicuous hilltop site for the Royal Observatory – a move he may have regretted later for its effect on the symmetry, for it was Wren, helped by Hawksmoor and Vanbrugh, who drew the whole thing together in a scheme of masterly grasp from 1696 to 1702. With its colonnades, its courtyards progressively narrowing as they recede from the river, its fine baroque domes (one over the chapel, one over the Painted Hall) and the Queen's House beyond, the effect is of fine detail cleverly subordinated to overall order.

The best way to Greenwich is by launch from Westminster or the Tower; river traffic now is mostly light, its sounds those of launch commentaries and the coaches' or coxes' instructions to the rowing eights. Once there, one should cross the river by the foot tunnel to the leafy pleasure garden opposite. This is the perfect place to contemplate Wren's and Jones's fine works, and much more peaceful than the grassy and slippery slopes of Greenwich Park which rise beyond them, down which the local children toboggan in August on squares of cardboard. The red ball on Wren's red-brick observatory still drops every day at one, a primitive but effective time signal for shipping and any clockmakers still left in Clerkenwell.

Greenwich: the Royal Naval Hospital

London's dockland

The great nineteenth-century docks which lined the banks upstream from Greenwich have vanished and the resultant desolation makes a sorry sight. The docks gave the whole of east London its *raison d'être* though, as part of the bargain, they also gave it the earliest and worst of its slums. Already in 1730 there were more people in Stepney than in Bristol; the cutting of the big nineteenth-century docks increased the need for living space while reducing the land available for it. In 1850 there were still no drains. Its slums too have vanished

following the war-time bombing and later redevelopment. They have left an empty plain of point blocks overlooking a waste of running-down or expired industry and the carcasses of the old warehouses. What can be done with it? All London's problems are here in a nutshell. There are various plans for re-invigoration, homing in over-optimistically on those inadequate panaceas leisure and tourism, or onto the fast-buck contractors' dream of an unwanted new airport. Visually the river spaces and the open skies are magnificent; they can be enjoyed from the nice riverside pubs and from the windows of the converted

warehouses, and in some places from the muddy foreshore itself. Echoes of traditional East End radicalism remain on dockyard walls and a few warehouses are still in use, agreeably spicy to nose and ear alike. Others have been boarded up and wired off prior to demolition, or suffer the worse indignity of being turned into commercialized legends. St Katharine's Dock is a strange mixture of good and bad, its approach guarded by teetering fibre-glass elephants, its quaysides stuck about with the fine cast-iron relics of Telford's demolished buildings – Doric columns, medallioned bollards, gas-lamp standards – as if they were garden gnomes.

18

Dock gateway, Wapping

Gateway, St Katharine's Dock

Bermondsey warehouses

TROOPS OUT OF IRELAND + WAPPING

Wapping Wall

Oliver's Wharf, Wapping

19

Wapping and Bermondsey

St Katharine's Dock was the smallest of the
London docks and the nearest to the City. It sits
on the site of the Hospital of St Katharine, an
old religious foundation; the soil that was dug
out to make the dock was used to raise the
marshy bits of what we now know as Belgravia.
Its East Dock contains a fine museum of ships.
The vessels range from a sturdy tug and the
archetypal 'dirty British coaster', the *Robin*, to a
lightship, a schooner and Scott's *Discovery*: a
romantic yet curiously out-of touch vessel.
Nearby is the *Cambria*, one of the lovely Thames
spritsail sailing barges, worked by a man and a
boy only, which used to be a familiar feature of
the river; others shelter elsewhere in the dock
or are tied up in the river alongside it.

Opposite is the river frontage which includes
Courage's old brewery, and just behind it the
remarkable brick-and-iron canyon of Shad
Thames. No one is about except caretakers,
now called security men, and film researchers.
In its heyday it must have been a labyrinthine
warren of activity: in decay, the rusting bridges
and cat-walks and crumbling brickwork
sprouting ferns and willow herb, it is still
astonishing: one of the key sights of London.
It should be seen quickly before it is pulled
down, as a reminder of how Londoners' working lives used to be lived. In this setting the
name Curlew Street seems ironic, yet it is not a
total misnomer, for only yards away a
crested grebe still bobs on the tideway.

Barge 'Cambria' and coaster 'Robin'

Shad Thames, Bermondsey

Blackfriars and Cannon Street

The railway engineers often marred honest
practicality with earnest pomposity. Blackfriars
railway bridge is a typical example, grand
Tuscan composite piers carrying girders much
too unassuming to match. As with all bridges,
its proportions change completely with the tide.
Beyond it is Bankside Power Station, built
opposite St Paul's amid a chorus of protest in
the mid-fifties but doing far less harm to the city
skyline than most of the unchallenged
additions since then.

Blackfriars railway bridge

On the north side, a good chunk of the Victorian riverside with its grand vista and telling detail is still intact. Here is one of the few remaining distant views of St Paul's not yet blocked by new building but framed instead by the grimy and theatrical towers of Cannon Street Station. Just beyond is a bit of Dickensian detail, the Bill-Sykes-type stairs down to the mud and the lighters. None of these things have been preserved on purpose or tarted up for the tourists. They are real.

Cannon Street Station

Southwark and the City bank

The south bank of the Thames from Bermondsey upstream still presented until quite recently a more or less continuous façade of warehouses. This is being transformed with alarming speed into an equally unbroken strip of office buildings. Just above London Bridge, on one of the likeliest sites for the Roman river crossing, old, recent and brand-new sit side by side, but still just leave a gap through to the south bank's finest medieval building, Southwark Cathedral. It looks neat, model-like, and fragile, a left-over from the past; but then so now does Pickford's Wharf, one of the few remaining old Southwark warehouses, romantic (to our eyes at least) in its height and history, grimy and magnificent in decline.

St Pauls and the Nat West Tower from Bankside

Southwark Cathedral and Pickford's Wharf

Seen looking north from Bankside, St Paul's is now backed and flanked by taller buildings and distinguished more by its dome than by any particular size or isolation. It survives of course very well. But from here Wren's fine church spires have become mere periscopes – several of them, including St Nicholas Cole Abbey, St Mary Somerset and St Mary-le-Bow, may be seen disconsolately poking up. St Benet, Paul's Wharf, is currently more fully visible; it shows Wren in his other idiom, brick-and-stone, familiar from Hampton Court and Chelsea Hospital but unusual for him in the City. The riverside buildings on either side of St Benet are a horrid and undistinguished mishmash from the journeyman days of post-war building, bounded by provincial horizons and with none of the style and command of the newer high blocks around Leadenhall Street. Visually it is a disaster because the rich and fascinating muddle left by the Victorians, who knew no better, has been replaced by what we, with our resources and techniques, should and could easily have ordered properly. It makes a sterile view for the Bankside pub and the children who fish on the foreshore.

King's Reach

The best view of the City and the Thames is seen looking east across King's Reach, from Hungerford or Waterloo Bridge or from the National Theatre terraces. It looks good in any light and provides one of the many incidental delights of going to the National. From here St Paul's still occupies the centre of the stage and its newer neighbours keep their distance. The offices along the Victoria Embankment towards Blackfriars are decently subordinated, and the Barbican flats stand apart, grouped as if watching like Henry Moore's trio of war-time London women. The NatWest Tower is tucked away out of sight and the shipping on the river adds life in the foreground.

As the National's evening performances draw near, Lasdun's terraces fill with visitors, and dancers and musicians join the pavement-level clothes stalls and booksellers. People enjoy strolling along the waterside and the young plane trees frame Somerset House and the City buildings beyond. It is a pleasant place where the opportunities offered by the river and by London itself have been made the most of.

King's Reach and the National Theatre

27

County Hall and Westminster

Significantly, County Hall is built on the site of a factory (the Coade Stone Works), Parliament on that of a palace. From these opposed seats of power separated by the river, national and local government confront one another like two old battleships, one pursing its lips and firing the torpedoes while the other, though doomed and sinking, goes down cheekily with all its heavy guns still firing. Giant business in the guise of Shell Centre stands impassive next door to County Hall as its products purr steadily upstream in tankers past the scruffy supply barges with their crates of beer and coke for the river boats. One is reminded here how much the river curves about: even when you can no longer see it, its serpentine course is discernible if you watch the big military helicopters that periodically lumber up and down it. Looking back, the City seems now to have swung round behind Shell, and St Paul's makes a final appearance before slipping out of sight behind the London Weekend Tower.

County Hall from the Victoria Embankment

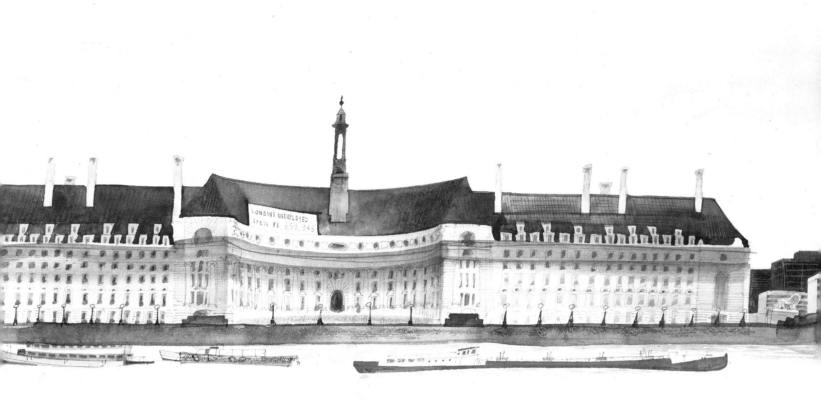

The best place to look at the Houses of Parliament is from the Albert Embankment opposite; indeed, the frontage is so long that you really have to walk along it to take it in properly. Thus observed, it seems curiously inconsistent: completely symmetrical up to waist height, resolutely asymmetrical above in its two dramatic verticals, the Victoria Tower and the Clock Tower housing Big Ben. It was only when drawing it that I noticed the forest of minor spires: they contained the Victorian central heating ducts.

After most of the old Palace of Westminster was burnt down in 1834, there was a competition to design a new one in gothic or Tudor style: it established gothic as the Christian Victorian norm. Two men of vastly different views collaborated on it, Charles Barry conceiving the whole thing and Augustus Welby Pugin supplying the excellent gothic detail inside and out, and even at the outset drawing it all sufficiently temptingly to win Barry the competition. Carrying it all through was hard work for them both: Barry died of worry and overwork and Pugin in Bedlam madhouse.

29

The Houses of Parliament from the Albert Embankment

Battersea and Hammersmith

Up-river from Vauxhall Bridge the great pre-war landmark is Battersea Power Station, 1929–55. Even before it was complete, while it stood for years like an up-ended three-legged table, it served as a symbol of the Romance of Power, its plumes of white smoke curling up like cottonwool against the sky, its massiveness relieved by careful modelling within the expanses of brickwork. When its generating days were almost over it was very properly declared a listed building. This meant that however ruinous to repair and maintain, it could not be pulled down. Following a competition to discover or invent a use for it, it seems likely to suffer the ignominy of ending up as a Leisure Park with space-age rides and similar attractions.

Battersea Power Station

Next to the power station is Chelsea Bridge, 1934, the first of three suspension bridges of which Albert Bridge, 1873, is the best-known and best-looking, but Hammersmith Bridge, 1884–7, the oddest. Its cast-iron structure and decoration are in a curious mixture of styles (part Frenchified, part squashed Tuscan). It suspends a pedestrian deck outboard of the roadway with a nice varnished guard-rail and benches on which you can sit and watch the sun set over Chiswick. It affords early proof (none is lacking today) that the best engineers do not necessarily make the best architects. Sir Joseph Bazalgette, who built it, was certainly one of London's greatest engineers; his masterpiece was the Victoria Embankment, part flood barrier, part by-pass, part underground railway, part sewer: a truly splendid achievement. A monument to him stands on the Embankment near Hungerford Bridge.

From the north end of Hammersmith Bridge you can reach the Mall with its pubs and intricate iron balconies. From the south end you can begin one of the prettiest strolls in London, the woodland riverside walk up the towpath to Barnes Bridge. Dinghies sail here – one filled up and sank unconcernedly as I walked past, but its occupants were instantly rescued by launch. There are fine views across to the terraces and riverside houses of Hammersmith and Chiswick, and leafy reflections that look like Corot's paintings.

Hammersmith Bridge

Chiswick and Mortlake

At the far end of Chiswick Mall a brick causeway slopes away through the mud into the water. Beside it a barge, a small tug boat and a lighter are tied up, seemingly by electric cable: each boat similar to others still at work on the river or in the St Katharine's Dock collection, though here converted into dwellings and their decks into gardens. The river has narrowed though the tide is still strong and the water muddy; the docks and the flood barrier belong to another world. The peace is disturbed only by the oarsmen on the tideway. Chiswick Eyot, the first of the upstream islands, stands green and willowy nearby, abreast of the Georgian waterfront houses of Chiswick Mall; yet only a stone's throw inland is the Hogarth Roundabout and the relentless M4.

Chiswick ferry

Maltings and pub, Mortlake

The riverside by the brewery at Mortlake makes me think of a provincial port like Sharpness or Wisbech, or the tall maltings on the Stour at Mistley which also, like the brewery, look like an isolated nineteenth-century left-over. It isn't as tall as it looks: each of the eight floors is only just high enough for a man to stand, raking and turning the damp barley. But it is impressive all the same, and enlivened on purpose by the touches of red brick over the windows and accidentally by the blue tie-beam plates that now clamp it all together. Such buildings, being for storing rather than processing, look peaceful, like high-stacked barns, not noisily industrial; and it would be easy to think that the Thames simply begins to subside here into its rural past. Eventually of course it does, more or less, but not before traversing many miles of built-up suburbia where the open spaces are playing fields, golf courses and reservoirs, and the shaded pools lie under wide concrete bridges.

The City and the East End

The City is the oldest bit of London, but often looks the newest. It is also the most concentrated, crammed as close as it can get to the river with no parks and few open spaces. As Britain's commercial and financial heart (or head), it is successful and prestigious and clearly very good at providing the kind of services in which it specializes. To judge by its prosperous-looking architecture, it seems to do very well out of whatever predicament the country at large finds itself in: a sort of Hong Kong, waiting to see what is going to happen and how best it can be turned to account.

Apart from the Tower, the bits of Roman-cum-medieval wall and the confused ground-plan, nothing of the old City survived the Fire. So the visible City really begins with Wren, and since City inertia or petty-mindedness thwarted his ideas as town-planner, Wren here means St Paul's and the smaller City churches he was charged to rebuild. Even now, depleted by demolition and bombing or simply outstripped by newer and taller upstarts, these churches are a remarkable and fascinating bunch, inside and out. One needs to prowl about a bit for a good viewpoint: many of them are well-hidden, and indeed to recapture the effect Wren sought, of tall church steeples rising like sentinels above a sea of lower buildings, one has now to go east of the City and look instead at the fine steeples built by his assistant Hawksmoor in Stepney, Spitalfields and Commercial Road, Limehouse.

The East End still forms a sort of backyard to the City. It remains in various ways a region where one can see people and industry at less of a remove than in the smart and prosperous City, and still sense in some degree how the City must have looked and felt before the war changed it all. After Wren, the City rather hung fire in the eighteenth century; the old houses were cleared off London Bridge, the Guildhall refaced and the Mansion House built, but it was only in the nineteenth century that Wren's City really began to get submerged by the rampaging explosion of commercial and industrial buildings which has left it, despite today's developments, still largely Victorian in flavour. Its notional core, in front of the Bank, the Mansion House and the Royal Exchange, may be an anti-climax as a central point in the City, but it is a notable collection of nineteenth-century buildings, despite the traffic and the backdrop of the new Stock Exchange and the NatWest Tower. The great markets, the warehouses and wharves, the railway stations and the bridges are nineteenth-century too, as are the great institutions of the law courts which grew up under the City's wing but were kept just outside its boundary like the great monastic institutions of an earlier age. These Victorian buildings are often of great beauty, like the Venetian-inspired office façades in Eastcheap, the repetitive façades of Queen Victoria Street, and the red-brick cathedral Waterhouse built in Holborn for the Prudential.

Such institutions all belong to a time when London felt itself to be, and indeed briefly was, the most important place in the world. All of them are good to draw. But I can't be bothered to draw their stuffy twentieth-century successors until they get 'modern': I really dislike the Empire architects, even when they are as prestigious as Lutyens and his one-time collaborator Baker, bringing up their Corinthian columns like big bombastic guns to ennoble the offices of Finsbury Circus and the banks of Poultry, or to ruin Soane's fine Bank of England. And the early post-war building, filling the blitz gaps like a dentist working with new and unfamiliar materials, also turns me right off: muddles of brick, stone, bronze, glass and coloured metal, succeeded by the overblown clip-on Festival of Britain eclecticism that now disfigures London Wall. Lately though, better architects have got a look in, so that the City's new centre of gravity off Leadenhall Street has well-built and confident buildings, like Commercial Union, the Deutsche Bank, and maybe in time Richard Rogers' new Lloyds, to give the whole place style and authority. The new City is certainly spectacular: the reflected sky in the all-glass façades, and the undulating play of light and shade as cloud shadows scurry up and down the sides of the tower blocks, are new and surprising sights, as are the office lights beginning to gleam out from the tall glass slabs as the afternoon light fades. All the same, the new tall City looks pretty thin, cautious and provincial by the standards of say mid-town Manhattan, but why shouldn't it? That's what it is.

St Bride's and the Barbican flats

Prospects from the City

These four drawings were made from the
top of a Fenchurch Street high-rise office block.
Looking north, the new City looks eager,
businesslike and rich; the skyscrapers have
lifted themselves free of the Wren church
towers and the Victorian and Edwardian offices,
and the newer they are, the better they look.
Richard Rogers' new Lloyds however is a
present yet to be unwrapped.

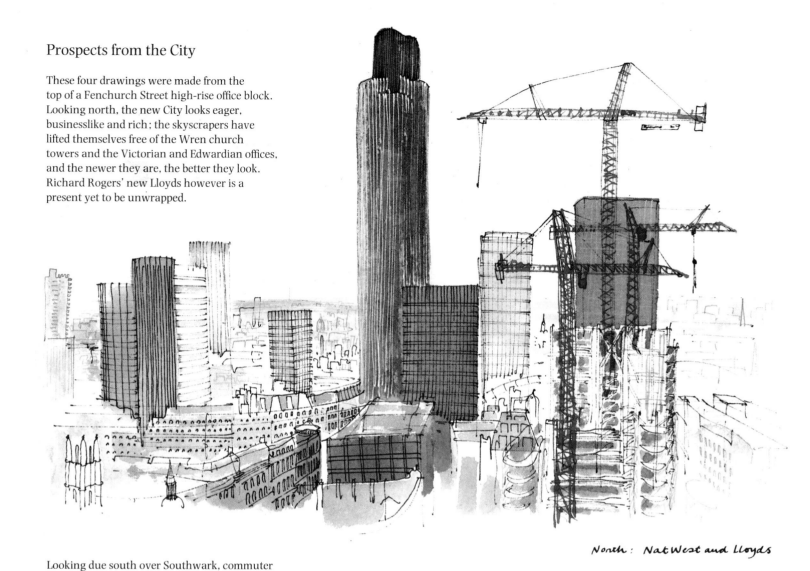

North: Nat West and Lloyds

Looking due south over Southwark, commuter
London stretches away flat and vast towards
Sydenham and the Crystal Palace mast. Just
over the river a few last warehouses are coming
down; old landmarks like Southwark Cathedral,
the railways enmeshing it, even London
Bridge itself, look minor beneath Guy's Hospital.
Down below, Lower Thames Street engulfs
Billingsgate and three Wren masterpieces.

36

South: towards Sydenham

To the east, London looks much more of a problem. The gleaming Thames snakes from the distant Barrier through the empty and ravaged Port of London, lying there waiting for a new role; already the biggest new building in sight is a hotel, the biggest space a sports centre. Most of this scene used to be under the sway of the old Port of London Authority, whose fine building (left of the Tower) now houses an insurance company. The concentric walls of the Tower look from up here like a toy or a soldier's sand-table model.

East: Towards the Isle of Dogs and Blackheath

Looking west, the other London – Westminster – seems an irrelevance, its spires hidden away out of sight and out of mind behind the Bankside Power Station. The West End is marked by Centre Point and the Post Office Tower. Nearer at hand King William Street cuts through the medieval city muddle. Seen from the directors' suite, London looks as it might to an approaching missile: beautiful and vulnerable.

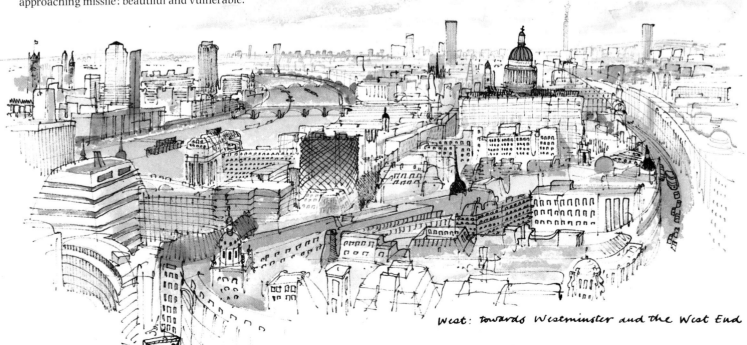

West: towards Westminster and the West End

Emperor Trajan and Wall, Tower Hill.

The Roman and medieval City

The Roman wall, built in the second century AD and almost two miles long, enclosed the settlement to landward; and since it was kept in repair again in medieval times, it shaped the City. The Romans were the first to realize that London had no stone to build with, and to put matters right. The wall was made of flat red tile-like bricks and Kentish ragstone which was brought from the Medway by barge. One of these flat-bottomed stone barges sank at its moorings at Blackfriars and was found in 1962 during work on the Embankment. Its remains are in the Museum of London.

Various fragments of the wall remain, most spectacularly at Tower Hill where it is guarded by a nice but none too ancient-looking bronze statue of the Emperor Trajan. Foundations of a Roman river wall too have been discovered, but it was left to decay. If you climb down the metal ladder onto the foreshore at Queenhythe at low tide you can watch people with metal detectors digging in the black mud for Roman and medieval coins, and finding bits of piping. It looks cold and dirty. More interesting reminders of the early Middle Ages lie supine in Purbeck marble effigy on the floor of Temple Church: eight Knights Templar, looking all the more enigmatic for their bomb damage. The round church of 1185 is London's first gothic building.

Queenhythe near Southwark Bridge

Earls of Pembroke, Temple Church

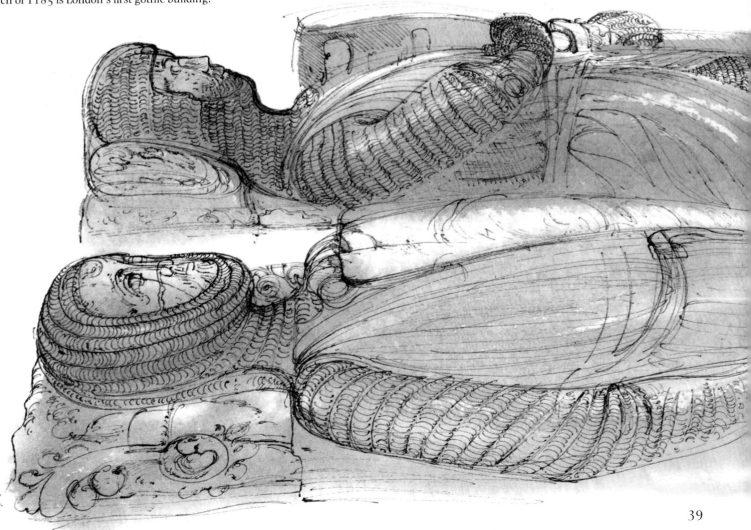

39

The Tower of London

The Tower is cleaner and prettier than it used to be, the whiter-than-white outer walls like foothills to the White Tower within. Some of it is now too clean to seem very ancient. But for all its newly restored walls and its jewels the Tower is a brutal place, stiff with relics of cruelty: suits of armour with grasshopper faces and beetle backs; prettily got-up cannon and other weapons to maim you; a place to chop your head off, a place called Traitors' Gate to drown you. Even the ravens are prisoners: they can only fly downhill. They croak resonantly once, twice, thrice; if it is cold, each croak appears as a little puff of misty breath and their head feathers plump out like a blow-dry. The walls of the narrow dark passageways in the White Tower are sharp with flints and rough stone; daily life must have been harsh. There is one very beautiful place in the Tower, the austere early Norman Chapel of St John, bare of almost all decoration save for its very plain capitals. Its few simple architectural forms – plain columns, round-headed arches, a barrel-vault, an aisle – are arranged without emphasis but to perfection.

Tower of London: Traitors' Gate

Tower of London: Chapel of St John in the White Tower

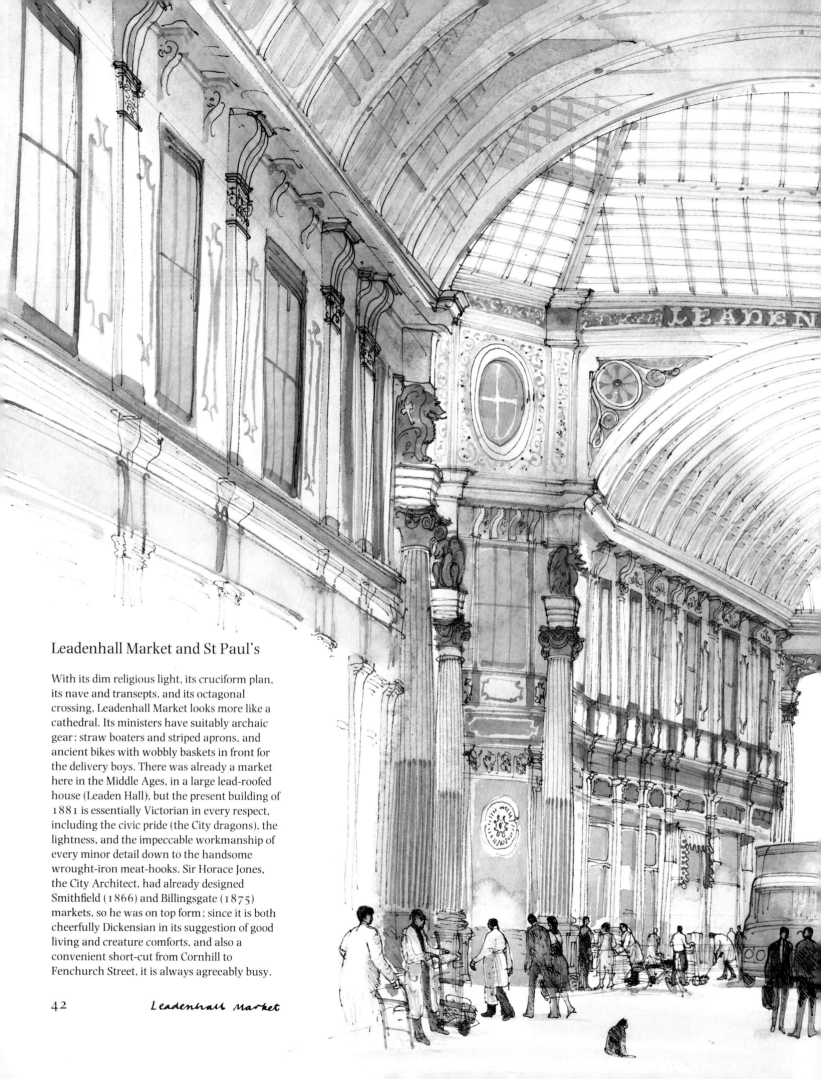

Leadenhall Market and St Paul's

With its dim religious light, its cruciform plan, its nave and transepts, and its octagonal crossing, Leadenhall Market looks more like a cathedral. Its ministers have suitably archaic gear: straw boaters and striped aprons, and ancient bikes with wobbly baskets in front for the delivery boys. There was already a market here in the Middle Ages, in a large lead-roofed house (Leaden Hall), but the present building of 1881 is essentially Victorian in every respect, including the civic pride (the City dragons), the lightness, and the impeccable workmanship of every minor detail down to the handsome wrought-iron meat-hooks. Sir Horace Jones, the City Architect, had already designed Smithfield (1866) and Billingsgate (1875) markets, so he was on top form; since it is both cheerfully Dickensian in its suggestion of good living and creature comforts, and also a convenient short-cut from Cornhill to Fenchurch Street, it is always agreeably busy.

42   *Leadenhall Market*

In the 1550s even St Paul's itself was likewise a short-cut and a market: the nave of the old gothic cathedral became St Paul's Walk, a street full of shopkeepers with their wares spread out on font and tombs. It must have looked almost as busy as it does in summer today. When Wren rebuilt the whole thing after the Fire he achieved the spatial effects he was after by two ingenious if theatrical illusions: an inner and an outer dome, and outer walls that enclose only empty space above the aisles. But however one may admire St Paul's, it is a hard building to *like* in the way one can like his smaller churches. There are some monstrously conceited tombs and some funny memorials, but too often the pretty details are simply swamped by the enormous size and ambitiousness. The whole thing took Wren thirty-five years; he went to see how it was getting on every week, 1800 visits. When as an old man he used to inspect the lantern, twice as high as Nelson's column, he had to be pulled up and down in a basket.

The nave of St Paul's   43

Christ Church, Newgate Street   St Mary-le-Bow, Cheapside   St Vedast, Foster Lane

Wren's churches and the Monument

With only an archbishop and a plain bishop to help him to redesign the City's burnt-down churches, Wren had a pretty free hand. His only limitations were the varying skills of the locally contracted craftsmen. This freedom shows up well in the inventiveness and command of all the buildings, and especially in their towers and spires; he built these last of all at the peak of his form. Opposite are three of those closest to St Paul's, which are also three of the most interesting.

All start off with simple square towers, but the upper stages vary greatly and show not only Wren's great skill but also his ability to work in different stylistic idioms. Of Christ Church, Newgate Street, only the steeple remains: it is square all the way up, including the square colonnade round the lantern, and apart from the pinnacles, everything is made up of familiar classical forms. At St Mary-le-Bow, or Bow Church, the lantern is round and topped by forms which here are of Wren's own devising. And at St Vedast, Foster Lane, the design is very subtle, the turrets above the square tower – the lower concave and the upper convex – giving beautifully modelled shadows. Here it is the strange new shape that matters most, not the derivation of the details.

The Great Fire still flames in a strange and brazen manner at the top of Wren's Monument to indicate where it broke out. The subject was not to Wren's taste: he would rather have had a statue of his friend Charles II. The Monument used to be the highest thing in sight, but now it is looked down on by the upwardly mobile offices all around it and from pavement level it is usually invisible. You can ascend the Monument by a very long spiral staircase: the view up or down the shaft is like looking through a rifled gun barrel. Boswell in 1762 was much frightened by the height, as was I, and he had only a rail to protect him. The canary cage was put there in 1842 after, over the years, six people had jumped off.

The Monument

Ceremony in the City

The City's pride takes two forms, flamboyant hype and majestic understatement. Its extrovert aspect appears in the Lord Mayor's magnificent coach, wheeled out of the London Museum once a year to take part in his or her procession. But by contrast, many of the City Livery Companies' Halls are built on minor streets, Skinners' Hall typically being still further hidden some distance behind its handsome street façade. The Guildhall itself is restrained and tucked away: you have to know where to look for it, and even then most of what you can see is Dance's curious 1788 frontage to the fifteenth-century building. And sometimes the grand gesture is itself upstaged by changing circumstances: the Mansion House architect Tite could hardly have foreseen it reduced as it now is to a mere ground-row to the new City.

The Lord Mayor's Coach

Royal Exchange and Commercial Union

Skinners' Hall, Dowgate Hill

The Guildhall

The horizontal City

Until the Fire, the City was wooden. Afterwards it became brick and stone and later iron; but it remained as before a horizontal place, the uniformity enforced by firm restrictions on height and on inflammable decoration, the only verticals the fine church spires here and there. The business of the place was carried on in houses, minimally adapted if necessary like the Fournier Street weavers' garrets, or in the halls of the City companies. Even the Bank of England started business this way, trading in

Mercers' Hall and Grocers' Hall until in 1734 it built itself not an office but a proper mansion of its own in Threadneedle Street. This also had to serve as an unofficial stock exchange. It was not until 1788 that Sir John Soane began to extend this mansion into a gracious banking building with a fine windowless protecting wall. This last is the only bit of Soane's work that has survived Herbert Baker's bloated and fuddy-duddy redevelopment in the 1920s and 1930s, which ripped out the splendid domed banking halls.

Even into the nineteenth century the new

engineers went on building horizontally, all the more effortlessly since new construction techniques meant that repeated units could just be conveniently fixed together *ad infinitum*, putting paid incidentally to the ancient pursuit of innately correct proportion. Henceforward more thought went into the parts than the whole, as both the agreeably patterned structures at the foot of the page suggest. But the repetition was only sideways. Storeys still, as before, got smaller as they got higher: no one in London had yet realized that you could bolt things together *upwards* as well.

Fournier Street, Spitalfields; Hawksmoor's rectory at right

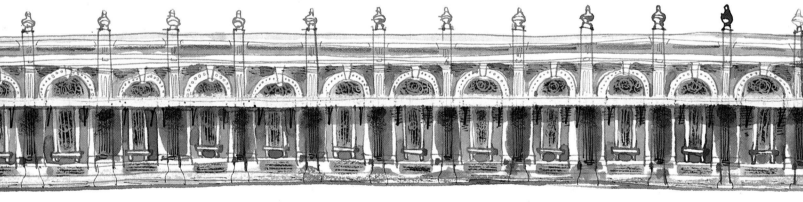

Smithfield Market

Albert Buildings, Queen Victoria Street (detail)

Ironmongers' Almshouses, Kingsland Road

Bank of England, Threadneedle Street

Liverpool Street Station

Blackfriars Bridge: balustrade

The vertical City

Thus, London never had either the urge or the means to go vertical in the last century; and even in this, though the technology was there, by-laws prevented it until the 1960s. Important buildings were distinguished by grandeur, not stature. Many of the uglier inter-war buildings owe their looks to attempts to thwart the regulations by, for example, building several storeys of office space into grotesquely deepened 'roofs'. These buildings, however enormous, still seem to be trying to look like little houses that have innocently grown a bit bigger. It was only in the 1950s that local-authority housing estates like Powell and Moya's Churchill Gardens and the LCC Architects' Alton East Estate began to get higher and higher, but by the end of the decade big slabs and point blocks were becoming widespread. Since then the City has acquired quite a clutch of them.

The first attempt to fit a group of such slabs into the City began in the early 1960s along London Wall, an area badly devastated in the blitz. At the time, the proposed buildings looked very tall and very modern with their steel and glass curtain walls. The earliest to be built have worn about as well as old cars of the same vintage: they sit there, old bangers now, as a battered testimony to poor standards and finish and above all to inexperience. But things have improved: the newest London Wall block, on the far left in the drawing, is well detailed and impressive, though to be fair its newness helps.

These buildings were envisaged as a sort of commercial edging to an area of new housing and cultural activity, the Barbican. Its most striking feature, a group of the three tallest blocks of flats in Europe, is 125 metres high and visible from all over London; the flats are recognizable by their height and their indented edges, like up-ended battlements. Externally they are of concrete like the rest of the Barbican Centre, a lavishly endowed but isolated region of desirable facilities: art gallery, concert hall, four cinemas, two theatres and a conservatory, the whole on ten levels. Bits of the old Roman-cum-medieval wall and fragments of several medieval churches crouch at its feet like good-luck charms.

Britain's tallest building, the National Westminster Tower of 1981, was built by Richard Seifert of Centre Point, the architect whose work for better or worse has changed the face of London more than any other individual's since Wren. Its tall metal ribs gleam seductively in different lights and there is nothing else here or anywhere else much like it. A more recent building still, the Deutsche Bank on Bishopsgate, belongs to a much more recognizable school, that of Mies van der Rohe. You cannot see into it: it is the ultimate black slab, like those menacing ones in Kubrick's 2001 whose appearance always heralded doom.

50

Office blocks on London Wall

Barbican tower block

National Westminster Tower

Deutsche Bank, Bishopsgate

City detail

Although the tall blocks have greatly changed the City skyline, much of what lies at their feet remains little altered. In any case one seldom sees very far at ground level in the City; apart from London Wall there are no grand vistas, and so one's eye is free to concentrate instead on curious and interesting detail, which abounds. It is best seen on foot; the distances are not great, and the traffic-free weekend is a good time if one does not mind the feeling of emptiness. At this pace, one can relish not only the City's quirks and not infrequent pratfalls, but also its moments of considerable beauty.

It is pleasant to wander along streets like Carter Lane or Ludgate Square with their arches and hoists, each hardly wide enough for a car; to see St Bride's steeple framed in a narrow warehouse vista, or standing out above the Pilgrim Street car-park, a bombed site which has been empty so long that it is now quite well-wooded. Another long-empty site nearby allows a uniquely uninterrupted view of Wren's brick St Benet, Paul's Wharf; even the famous view from Fleet Street of St Paul's and St Martin, Ludgate is half-masked by bridge and offices. Occasionally the new buildings show the old in an unexpected light, as when walking up Clement's Lane one is surprised to see *twin* spires on Wren's St Edmund the King, the right-hand one reflected in the glass and polished stone of some new offices. And quite frequently one sees cranes in a predatory attitude over some defenceless monument like St Botolph, Bishopsgate, whose parish hall carries two of the City's prettier bits of sculpture, 1821 Coade stone figures of charity children. Equally graceful foundling children stand outside St Andrew, Holborn; a fully dressed American philanthropist and a naked Grecian fountain goddess sit behind the Royal Exchange without communicating, and a whole pantheon of helmeted gods look down from the banking hall of the old National Provincial headquarters. This building, like the City of London Club opposite, was due for the chop to make way for the NatWest Tower; but the City planners, having thrown out the magnificent Coal Exchange without a backward glance, were suddenly stricken with remorse and capriciously reprieved these lesser treasures. Similar agonizing and second thoughts currently hang over the future of Mappin and Webb on the Mansion House Square site earmarked for the Mies van der Rohe tower block designed some twenty years ago. Mies was an excellent architect but his role here was also to supply the prestige necessary to impress the planners. But a building has not only to be conceived but also carried through, and Mies in the meantime has died.

Pilgrim Street car-park

St Benet, Paul's Wharf

St Bride's from Carter Lane

Ludgate Square offices

Clement's Lane

Fountain behind the Royal Exchange

Austin Friars

Ludgate Hill

Liverpool Street

Foundling

George Peabody

Bishopsgate

Masons' Avenue

Charity schoolchildren

Throgmorton Street and the City of London Club

The Mansion House and Mappin and Webb

Holborn and Gough Square

Fleet Street has been associated with printing and bookselling for almost five centuries and with newspapers and writers for half that. But many of the bigger papers are now off Fleet Street, in Gray's Inn Road, Farringdon Road or in Holborn, like the *Daily Mirror*, whose architecture is unhappily in the old banger league. Literary associations naturally abound. Dickens wrote *Pickwick Papers* over the road in Furnival's Inn, which then stood where Alfred Waterhouse's Prudential building does today, a magnificent red-brick gothic cathedral whose spires are now dwarfed by its shiny neighbours. Samuel Johnson lived and worked nearby in a fine seventeenth-century house in Gough Square, compiling his *Dictionary* with the help of six clerks in a businesslike attic workshop not unlike a weaver's garret. The domestic floors below are delightful, looking onto the square with nice glimpses through from one elegantly panelled room to another and hung with good pictures and prints of Johnson's circle. Journalists still work in Gough Square, but straight into the microphone in the LBC studios. My connections with this area have been firmly paper-and-ink based because of the wood-engraving blocks, tools and Japanese papers made or sold by Mr Lawrence high up on the top floor above Bleeding Heart Yard, off Greville Street. Mr Lawrence is well into his eighties and in 1984 was still going in every day to run the business. Dickens knew this well-hidden yard and described it minutely in *Little Dorrit*.

T. N. Lawrence and Son's workshop, Bleeding Heart Yard

Interior of Dr Johnson's house

Dr Johnson's house in Gough Square

Two Mirrors and the Prudential, Holborn

Hall of the Royal Courts of Justice

The Law Courts and Middle Temple

Legal London is partly inside the City, partly out; the Temple is in it but the Law Courts stand just outside, in the Strand. They were built in the 1870s by Street, on the site of old slums; the frustrations of the job killed him but the result is extremely impressive. About ten in the morning the great hall is a splendid sight, with its columns and vaulting, its hush and its picturesque gowned barristers like clergymen, actors or surgeons in an operating theatre; the whole scene is like a cathedral without the music. Here, bewigged barristers and plain-clothes solicitors meet their sometimes rather bemused clients, and shepherd them off through the gothic arched doorways to the many individual courts where anyone who cares to may watch the law in operation. These chambers, like side-chapels off the great nave, are soberly panelled but theatrically arranged. The stalls are occupied by the opposing legal teams, the gallery by the public, the orchestra pit by clerks and typists; uniformed usherettes at the sides guard the steps up to the raised stage onto which the three learned judges enter from backstage through arches left and right.

The Temple, south of the Strand, looks like an Oxford or Cambridge college, only bigger: the same grand architectural mixture, the same grassy courtyards, passages, archways and fountains and occasional venerable pokiness, even the same staircases with the names of the senior and junior occupants. Professional legal needs are met by various specialist shops and unspecialist pubs. There is a particularly nice-looking shop just behind the Law Courts; its elegant plastered façade and learned legal windows full of caricatures of judges surround the archway into New Square, which in turn leads on into Lincoln's Inn Fields.

Appeal court in session

Bookshop, New Square

Doorway, No. 2 Middle Temple Lane

Lincoln's Inn Fields with Lindsey House by Inigo Jones

Lincoln's Inn Fields

Lincoln's Inn Fields is an early instance of a developer, William Newton, pulling off a *coup* in the face of local opposition, from the people of Lincoln's Inn who would have preferred their pleasant fields to stay the way they were. The King appointed Royal Commissioners, of whom Inigo Jones was one, to protect their interests. But before long he had changed sides, and Newton's plans got off to a good start when in 1640 Inigo Jones built Lindsey House on the west side; it is a fine example of classical forms used with vigour and style rather than with timid correctness. The fields are still well-wooded with fine old planes and a curved metal one by Barry Flanagan.

Earlier sculpture fills Sir John Soane's Museum in the architect's own house on the north side of the square. It contains a curious, almost surreal conglomeration of classic ornament and fragments, and good drawings and paintings including much Hogarth. The magpie acquisitiveness and profusion of the contents do not fully reflect Soane's own restrained and extremely original style as an architect. This can just be seen behind all the bric-à-brac in the remarkable arched interiors.

Sir John Soane's Museum   Plane trees, Lincoln's Inn Fields   Trees by Barry Flanagan   59

The new City and Bunhill Fields

To get the City in perspective one must step back from it. A good vantage-point for this is the high-level walkway of Tower Bridge. From here one can see the old hundred-foot roofline of the Portland stone offices on Tower Hill; the taller but still pretty flat-footed brick and concrete of the early post-war rebuilding; and the increasingly skilful and assured steel and glass from the 1960s on. The first skyscrapers always have the best views. Later arrivals fare worse; they see only each other, and most buildings look rather scruffy when you look down on them; the water tanks, guard-rails and fire escapes that can be decently hidden from the pavement seem from above to have been thrown onto the roofs as carelessly as children's bricks. Unfortunately, the more severe and clean-cut the building, the more obtrusive these extranea.

The City from Tower Bridge

Bunhill (Bone Hill) Fields lies north of the
City; with Moorfields and Finsbury Fields it
formed the remnants of an earlier tract of
fenland outside the City walls. In 1549
cartloads of bones were brought here from the
St Paul's charnel-house. During the Great
Plague in 1665 a section of the fields was
walled in, but it was never used for plague
burials and never consecrated; it thus became
available for burying Nonconformists. There
are monuments here to Bunyan, Defoe and
Blake. Beneath the plane trees is a stone
landscape: serried ranks of near-illegible
gravestones with their simply shaped but varied
top edges, and the occasional grander tombs
like fat carp among the minnows.

Bunhill Fields

Fournier Street and Spitalfields

Wren's assistant Nicholas Hawksmoor built only one church in the City, but three very fine ones just outside in the East End. The most splendid is Christ Church, Spitalfields, ordered by the High Church Tories under the 'fifty new churches' Act in 1711 to quench Nonconformity in this factious district of free-thinkers and newly arrived Huguenots. He created a tall and slender yet commanding spire for the job. But despite even Hawksmoor, Nonconformism was too strong to be quelled. The French dug themselves in and set up flourishing silk businesses, the richest merchants and master weavers building the beautiful Georgian houses behind the church in Fournier Street. Their fine carved doorways and well-lit attic weaving rooms remain, though since then the district has changed hands radically more than once. The Georgian Methodist chapel of 1743 later became a synagogue and is currently the London Jama Masjid, the mosque for the Bangladeshi rag-traders who permeate Fournier Street and Brick Lane. Exotic foods fill to bursting the once restrained shop windows, just as jam-packed cutting and machining rooms fill the sedately fronted houses. Not much conforming here.

Spitalfields Market has flourished for three hundred years more or less unchanged, a reminder now of how Covent Garden looked until the early 1970s: cheeky, efficient and proud of itself. Like Fournier Street it is a curious mixture: flowers on the ancient wooden handbarrows, cabbage crates on the fork-lift trucks, Cockney overalls and Muslim caps in front of the shaded churchyard monuments. With the market pub on Hawksmoor's left and the wrought-iron gents down on his right, it all makes a good down-to-earth foil to his skilful baroque rhetoric.

Christ Church, Spitalfields

Fournier Street and Brick Lane details

Sunday flower market, Columbia Road

The East End markets

Petticoat Lane is the best-known of the street markets that flourish on the City's fringes. The general public are now a lot more exotic than the Cockney barrow boys, but the markets are always good value to look at, their barkers good to listen to but bad to cross. A few hot-dog stalls are tarted up to look American but in general there is no attention paid to 'image'. The display is minimal and the graphics are agreeably home-made, painstakingly written out between bouts of peanut-roasting. Packaging being non-existent, you pay merely for what you want plus the fun of a bit of real live face-to-face salesmanship. This of course is noisy: the hubbub makes a sharp contrast with the studious hush that on Saturdays hangs over the long-established second-hand bookstalls in Farringdon Road, where people browse through old books of engravings or ferret into boxes of dusty remnants.

Neither the Victorians nor the Edwardians liked the street traders, feeling no doubt that they were piratical freelances who threatened the Sunday-observing shop-keeping middle classes. The Victorians tried unsuccessfully to tempt them off the pavements into the handsome neo-gothic Columbia Market where bells chimed hymns every quarter hour. The Edwardians, made of sterner stuff, drove buses and fire-engines through the market streets in an attempt to dislodge the traders; but they could not. Columbia Road today is still a beautiful Sunday market for flowers and bedding plants, which attracts a clientele much more discriminating than the Petticoat Lane sightseers. The low buildings curving away on either side leave it open to the sky, and the plants and seedlings look fresh and lovely. It is lucky that no one managed to ban the costermongers from the streets, for scenes like these are easily the liveliest and the nicest-looking spectacles now left in the East End.

second-hand bookstalls, Farringdon Road

Chestnuts and jewellery, Petticoat Lane

Jellied eels and peanuts, Brick Lane

65

Off Rotherhithe Street

The Surrey Commercial Docks

The East End today

Costermongers and barrow boys, silk-weavers and the rag trade, ship-builders and furniture-makers all helped to make up the East End, and all had their own districts and centres. But the things that mattered most of all were the docks. At first these were merely stake-lined recesses cut in the earthy river banks, drying out and filling with each tide. Most ships anchored in the middle of the river and their cargoes were poled ashore by lightermen: much of it was stolen. So, early in the nineteenth century, the big wet docks were dug with heavy lock-gates to keep the tidal water in and tall brick walls

like fortresses to keep the thieves out. As the prospering docks grew ever bigger they squeezed the people who worked there tighter and tighter together in the dreadful undrained back-to-back squalor of the East End slums. Ironically this squeezing together only went vertical into point blocks in the 1960s, just at the moment when the docks stopped needing any space at all: container ships can unload quicker and at any tide further down the river at Tilbury or at ports like Felixstowe, and now the docks lie idle or filled in. South of the river in the old Surrey Docks you can only tell where they were by an occasional curving roadway and by the general air of desolation: quayside

derricks have given way to demolition cranes. But north of the river the lock-gates and the still water remain, the wharves dotted with men fishing. At the twin locks into Limehouse Basin, the Regent's Canal (and thus the whole canal system of the country) joins the river; it is in working order but the Limehouse Cut beside it is now a stretch of willow herb and shrubs between rows of sheds and watermen's houses. The old Billingsgate fish market has moved from the City to the West India Docks on the Isle of Dogs, beyond the wooden lock-gates that used to let in ocean-going liners and their cosmopolitan crews. The only things that sound foreign now are the café names.

Lock gates, West India Dock

Limehouse Basin, the Regent's Canal Dock

The old Limehouse Cut

Commercial Road

Big Ben

Westminster and St James's

Upstream from the City lies a beautiful but poignant region embracing four great palaces. St James's Palace, Buckingham Palace and the Palace of Westminster still stand. The ancient Whitehall Palace has almost vanished, replaced by or adjoining those interlinked and mutually sustaining institutions of Church (not yet wholly discarded), Monarchy and State: Abbey, Foreign Office, Downing Street, Horse Guards, Ministry of Defence and so on. This area is full of things to look at: the great Abbey with its kings and queens, statesmen and poets; King James's Banqueting Hall; the restrained house-fronts of Lord North Street, the shady avenues of the Mall, the long façade of Kent's Horse Guards; and the classical elegance and repose of the St James's clubs. And there are many quiet and more withdrawn spaces, such as Dean's Yard, Smith Square, and the beautiful Embankment Gardens. Government offices command the skyline of Whitehall, pretty ones from the nineteenth century, bigger and severer ones from the twentieth. But at the heart of it is the romantic Victorian silhouette of Westminster, all gothic spike and upward thrust; and indeed Big Ben has long been deservedly the familiar and almost universally accepted symbol of democracy itself.

Inside, the interior halls, stairways, passageways and chambers of the Palace look as if they were contrived with symbolism primarily in mind, with the gothic detailing, the frescoes, the panelling, the policemen and the reverence. It also has the air of a rather old-fashioned boys' public school, with its rituals, its prefects' rooms, its library and its gym, its matron and its statues of famous old boys; and its charges are carefully shielded from things best not known about or discussed. Of recent years, governments have grown increasingly secretive, even about the most important issues of the time. For example, neither the development of British nuclear weapons, nor the true nature of the arrangements under which the USA built up its nuclear bases in this country, were ever fully disclosed to Parliament or even to the Cabinet. Such secrecy compromises democracy. Big Ben was being cleaned when I drew it, giving the place an appropriately blinkered and muffled look.

Whitehall architecture is especially rich and resonant. Starting at Parliament Square and ignoring the Cenotaph, one sees on the left the splendidly self-confident and stylish Victorian buildings for the Treasury and the Foreign Office; Kent's Horse Guards from a century earlier; and opposite them and a century older still, Inigo Jones's Banqueting Hall, all that is now left of the Palace of Whitehall and a key building in the English adoption of civilized European style and standards. It used to be a dominant feature of Whitehall, but now it crouches miserably in the shadow of the Ministry of Defence building which stretches on as far as the old bank of the Thames. Just behind it, embedded in the lawn where the river bank used to be, are the steps down to the water that Wren built for Queen Mary, surrounded now by quaint statuary of service notables. The earlier ones like the swashbuckling General Gordon of 1887 were glamorized by clever sculptors working in a tradition that – judging by the lamentable recent statuary nearby – has gone for ever. More of the good old-fashioned sculpture of forgotten imperial giants and martial heroes stands forlornly about beneath the plane trees in the nearby Embankment Gardens and in Trafalgar Square and Waterloo Place, like ancient advertisements for vanished and unlamented products.

But there is more to this region of London than empty rhetorical nostalgia for the glories of Empire. In the magnificent gatehouse of St James's Palace and the elegance of Queen Anne's Gate there is hard evidence of a thriving and ingenious past; and if, under the arches of Hungerford Bridge, there lie today reminders of the harsh reality of Victorian values, there also exists in the chamber of the Commons a mechanism perfectly well able to put things right if it chose to.

The House of Commons

Parliament and the Abbey

The Palace of Westminster looks too much like the Abbey for its own good. Pugin is all too clearly borrowing dignity for the State from the Church, the expert in the business. But though Pugin's painstaking gothic detail is visible in profusion in the Lords and the Central Lobby, there is none in the Commons, a chamber without pretension to architectural style (and none too comfortable-looking either). Its visual blankness is a relief after the fusty pageantry of

St Stephen's Hall and the Central Lobby, for it concentrates the interest on what is really going on. And whereas for all its pomp and architectural splendour the Lords is venerably toothless, the Commons chamber – however dull visually – is a fascinating place when in action. The Commons is not such a bear garden as it sounds on the radio; it is in reality an interesting and unpredictable place where one can wander in and hear MPs' car allowances and Falklands peace negotiations debated without anyone pausing for breath.

The mutual propping-up of Church and State, real enough in the past if barely relevant now, manifests itself constantly over the road in the Abbey. The sculpture that expresses it is mostly of very high quality, but the earliest is the best of all: by the nineteenth century it has all begun to look a bit too easy and too complacent, like elegant but routine plugs for the *status quo*. Many of these stand in Statesmen's Aisle, including three elegant generations of Cannings, one Disraeli and one Gladstone, all on marble columns cut down to

the size of polished stone soap-boxes. (But compare the depressingly inept sculptures of more recent statesmen in Parliament Square and in the Houses of Parliament.) The masterly structure and clarity of the Abbey, seen purely as a medieval building, are remarkable. Its uniformity of style, unique at a time when great buildings almost always developed more radically as they grew, was imposed by the great master mason Henry Yevele; but, apart from the work that one can see all around, there is no monument to him.

Statesmen's Aisle, Westminster Abbey

Dean's Yard and Smith Square

The visitors' way out of the Abbey leads into
Dean's Yard, a quiet and pleasant haven
otherwise easy to miss. You can hear the Abbey
bells chime and watch the Westminster
scholars running about or playing games. The
fine west towers of the Abbey rise beyond it.
They are not, as one might think, more of the
work of Henry Yevele, but that of Nicholas
Hawksmoor being medieval in the 1730s: a few
tell-tale baroque quirks can be spotted, over the
roundel for instance. By then, Thomas Archer's
proper baroque church of St John (now a
concert hall) in nearby Smith Square was also
complete. It was the dearest of the fifty new
churches ordered by the Tory Parliament in
1711, and it looks it. Its towers, very different
from Hawksmoor's, look down on the perfect
early-Georgian houses of Lord North Street,
where very rich MPs like to live today.

Dean's Yard and Westminster Abbey

St John, Smith Square and Lord North Street 73

Horse Guards Parade

Buckingham Palace and the Horse Guards face each other across St James's Park. The Horse Guards is infinitely the better-looking. William Kent designed it at the end of his life and it has all the assurance and command of a late work. The Palladian rustication and the pyramid roofs on the two central pavilions are Kentish features; and the shallow arches unify and enlarge the effect of the windows. Kent designed it to an E-shaped plan, with projecting wings and a central block, itself E-shaped; the projections of the white stone seem to take on the broken light-and-shadow effects of a line of chalk cliffs partly fallen away and further eroded at the base. It is lovely in any light; but after rain, with the sparkle of the sea of official cars and the calm reflections and sandy pools of the rain-soaked and gravelly beach, the marine effect is memorable.

This fine parade ground used to be the Whitehall Palace tiltyard, and reviews, parades, and such ceremonies as Trooping the Colour have always been held here. In 1540 Henry VIII attracted knights from all over Europe to compete at a tournament on this site. Architecturally and spatially, the Horse Guards ranks with Greenwich as one of London's greatest set-pieces. Unfortunately, Whitehall top brass are now allowed to park here in their droves, so that the normal weekday spectacle still looks like a tournament, or at any rate a war game.

The Horse Guards from the Guards Memorial

The Embankment Gardens by Whitehall Court

Embankment Gardens and the MoD

The Embankment Gardens, drowsy and complacent beneath the spires of Whitehall Court, look like a shot from the titles for a Raj serial. The grass is parched like a *maidan* and even the Indian bean trees with their big leaves and hanging pods look imperial. But the empire-builders stand on pedestals and the lower orders are white.

Where the gardens lie, the river used to flow; the Palace of Whitehall stood at the water's edge in the middle distance. Nothing of it remains but Inigo Jones's Banqueting Hall and

the prettily curving steps which Wren built so that Queen Mary could board the Royal Barge; you can see them just by the corner of the Ministry of Defence. Inigo Jones's intelligent and literate work has been completely swamped by this colossal Stalinist block, a building designed before the first war yet only built after the second, by which time the Edwardian aesthetic of its absurd classical colonnade and beach-hut pavilions up at penthouse level had been totally exploded. A false note from yet another period is struck by the lumpish nudes stuck up by the front doors above the official cars. These grotesque figures,

affecting a style youthful in the thirties but already academic and stuffy by the fifties, signify 'Earth' and 'Water'. For a British ministry now reduced to public relations chores for American cruise missiles it is powerless to control, 'Hot Air' and 'Fire' would seem more fitting elements. But absurdity is the keynote here.

The price we pay for such national priorities may be seen at the other end of the Embankment Gardens, in the train-rumbling gloom under Hungerford Bridge. Londoners tend to avoid or accept this scene, but visitors seem to react with the same kind of shock one would feel in a Calcutta slum.

The Ministry of Defence, House Guards Avenue

Embankment Place under Hungerford Bridge

Queen Anne's Gate and the Mall

Westminster's other perfect early-eighteenth-century street is quite near, just off St James's Park. Queen Anne's Gate has a very good statue of its queen and beautiful houses with fine brown brickwork and tall, well-proportioned windows; but its prettiest features are its finely carved doorways, their porches dripping with pineapples, foliage and faces. The nice thing about these Queen Anne's Gate houses is their human scale: one can enjoy the brick patterning and the lovely carving because everything in the street is close enough to see just as clearly as one would see the face of somebody opening one of the doors. By contrast, the scale of the tall grey Home Office building on the corner is appropriate to a building which can be seen from the far side of St James's Park, which it dominates; and the curious rubber-tyre swelling near the top serves to distinguish it from other straight-sided slabs. But when such large-scale shape-making gets down to pavement level, it relates to the Queen Anne's Gate houses about as well as a car showroom to a drawing-room. Its architect, Sir

Basil Spence, who also designed the Household Cavalry Barracks off Knightsbridge, cannot be said to have done much for London's skyline: these two tall but undistinguished buildings stand prominently at the edge of the two Royal Parks, just where they do most harm. Indeed, the Home Office can still be seen from the Serpentine bridge, spoiling the famous distant view of Westminster.

On the opposite side of the park is the Mall, laid out by Charles II with two rows of trees on each side, forty years earlier than Queen Anne's Gate. It was for long a favourite walking- and meeting-place as well as an alley for playing *paille maille*, a kind of croquet. It must have been pleasant: it looks pretty in the old prints. It was shorter then than now. In the early 1900s it was lengthened and greatly widened into a grand processional route between the new Queen Victoria Memorial and the Admiralty Arch; both the adjoining parks lost land to it in the process. It provides London's one grand vista, and in the spring it looks very pretty, even though for six days a week it is simply a motorway. But on Sundays it is a proper mall again, for people only.

Queen Anne's Gate and the Home Office

Plane-tree avenue by the Mall

House in Queen Anne's Gate

The gates of Buckingham Palace

The Palace and Number Teh

The general impression created at the gates of
Buckingham Palace is good-natured and
relaxed. The gates are open, friendly policemen
chat and pose for snaps, the palace brougham
trots in and out with messages, and everyone
can look their fill and leave satisfied at having
seen where the Queen lives.

Unless you are a schoolchild or work there
you can no longer walk up Downing Street to
look at Number Ten, and from beyond the
heavy metal crush barriers at the Whitehall
end it is hard even to tell which house it is.
However prudent this is, the impression here is
both authoritarian and nervous.

The barriers of Downing Street

St James's Palace

When Henry VIII gave away or sold the monasteries, he kept for himself the land on which stood St James's Hospital for leper maidens and built St James's Palace in its place. It served as the home of kings and queens of England for twice as long as Buckingham Palace has. Henry VIII's splendid gatehouse survives, black and commanding, as the focal point of St James's Street. It is best seen from fairly close quarters, thus avoiding the view of the tall offices rising above it beyond the park. Round the corner in the courtyard opposite Marlborough House and the Inigo Jones chapel one can see the guard being changed amid less of a crush than at the Horse Guards or Buckingham Palace. Friary Court is newer than it looks, rebuilt after an 1809 fire; it is a good early example of nostalgic Tudor, its quiet arcades disturbed only by the chimes of the gatehouse clock.

St James's Street has several fine clubs, notably White's, Boodle's and Brooks's, and some handsome old shop-fronts such as Lock's and Berry Brothers and Rudd's. But the scene has been lately sullied by the vulgarly self-assertive bent-metal office building at No. 66, on the corner of St James's Place. This does about as much for the overall St James's Street scene as the Sun Alliance's sponsored bent-metal litter-bin opposite Henry VIII's palace. Both are put to shame by the distinguished *Economist* offices up the street, which show how a good modern building can actually enhance the whole scene.

Sun Alliance's litter-bin

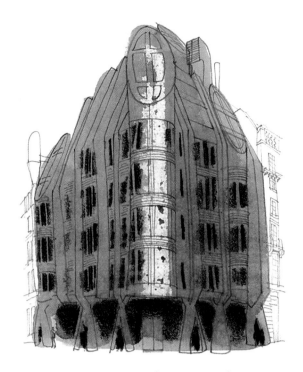

Offices, 66 St James's Street

Berry Brothers and Rudd's shop, St James's Street

Friary Court, St James's Palace

The gatehouse, St James's Palace

Trafalgar Square

Nelson's column does not work: Corinthian
capitals were meant to hold up entablatures,
not admirals. So the finest monument in
Trafalgar Square is not Nelson's (whose giddy
predicament would better suit Harold Lloyd)
but King Charles I's. This magnificent figure sits
on horseback at the top of Whitehall, on a
pedestal supposed to have been designed by
Wren and carved by Grinling Gibbons and
certainly handsome enough to have been. The
bronze figure was ordered to be melted down
after the King's execution, and the brazier
appointed to do so made a fortune by selling
souvenirs supposedly cast from the bronze; but
he had really only buried it in his garden, and
dug it up again later. The best-loved and most-
used sculptures in the square are Landseer's
splendid lions, much climbed on by children.

Trafalgar Square and the National Gallery

To the right is the fine steeple of St Martin-in-the-Fields, built in 1722–4 by James Gibbs who designed the equally pretty St Mary-le-Strand. The north side of the square is occupied with dignity by the National Gallery; but the space to its left (beyond the large lamp-standard) is due to be filled by the much-debated Gallery Extension. One might think that the best way to build such an extension is the seemly and innocuous way adopted up the road by the Royal Opera House, so successfully that you cannot tell where the old ends and the new begins. But this was expensive; and the National Gallery (i.e. the Government) could only afford its own one by getting someone else to do the paying. So the gallery trustees naively set about getting their Extension for free by having it popped in along with a Trafalgar Square prime-site office block that would be given (only for a mere 128 years or so) as a *pourboire* to some altruistic and well-connected developer. The idea was to get the seventy-nine cleverest architects in the world to put up some suggestions and see who was best. The trouble was not so much that no one liked any of them, but that Prince Charles didn't either, speaking of monstrous carbuncles and so on. These properly belong on the faces of the instigators, whose credulity consisted not so much in thinking that an Extension of Trafalgar Square calibre could be got for free as in supposing that the free-ness wouldn't show. This is a shaming predicament for the guardians of Constable and Turner, and for the land of Nelson. One would pause to reflect before paying for the upkeep of the Queen's pictures by letting someone build an office block in the front courtyard of Buckingham Palace.

Waterloo Place and Pall Mall

The handsomest column in London is the Duke of York's in Waterloo Place, nine years older and twenty feet shorter than Nelson's but much better-looking, and tall enough to keep the Duke – a much-loved commander-in-chief who died owing £2 million – out of reach of his creditors. Below it in Waterloo Place, nineteenth-century ideas of war, honour, privileged elegance and the benign power of patrician reform stand thick on the ground. The monuments are beautifully arranged and well-sculpted. Indeed, the general effect of this southern conclusion of Nash's triumphal route from Regent's Park to the vanished Carlton House is masterly: a skilfully arranged open space which nowadays leads on over Pall Mall and down the Duke of York's Steps into St James's Park. Nash's improving hand can also be seen in the nearby Royal Opera Arcade, a tunnel of elegant shop-fronts changing what had previously become a run-down and squalid area into London's first shopping arcade

The Royal Opera Arcade

Waterloo Place and the Duke of York's column

Carlton Gardens

86

Next along Pall Mall to Burton's Grecian-looking Athenaeum are two clubs more like Florentine *palazzi*. The Travellers' and the Reform were both designed by Barry; he cut his teeth on the first but excelled himself on the second. It is a handsome building, with a bewildering profusion of mirrored alcoves or openings through into adjoining rooms, you hardly know which; and there are fine paintings and busts of Cobden, Bright and other Reformers, and the smoking-room in which Phileas Fogg laid his famous bet. The club's dining-room looks out onto the fine plane trees of Carlton Gardens, but its most striking feature is the magnificent galleried courtyard which Barry was reluctantly persuaded to glaze over. The two-tiered columns round this courtyard give it a touch of *ante-bellum* Charleston, and the first-floor gallery between them gives a bird's eye view of one of London's most splendid interiors. The combination of gilded magnificence, good architecture and sculpture and conspicuous leisureliness makes the Reform visually the perfect club.

The Reform Club

Pall Mall with the Athenaeum, the Travellers' and the Reform Clubs

St James's Square

The town square originated in France and Italy but was perfected in London. The basic plan is quite elastic: there are several possible variants, and they are seldom carried out completely symmetrically. In Inigo Jones's Covent Garden Piazza of 1631, two approach roads led to the corners, two to the middle; in Bedford Square, *c.* 1775, the roads again lead into its corners, as they also do in Belgrave Square of 1825,

though here they approach diagonally, greatly altering the feel of the square. St James's Square, of 1665, was one of the earliest, and was – unlike most of them – geometrically a true square. It has three formal vistas pointing at its centre, where there is a good bronze statue of William III on horseback. Although for its first hundred years or so a house here was the best address in London, it is almost all offices or clubs now; the only house still privately owned is the Libyan People's Bureau.

One gets the best sense of the square's original plan when the trees are bare, showing how the original uniformity has been broken and the roofline stealthily raised, first by building within the roof and then, having got away with that, by adding more storeys. In summer it is densely leafy, and the buildings are masked out. It is perhaps nicest of all at lunchtime on a warm autumn day, when picnickers drift in from their work in ones and twos as the leaves are beginning to fall.

St James's Square looking north

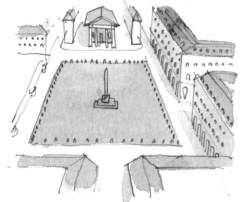

Covent Garden: the piazza

Belgrave Square

Bedford Square

Regent's Park: Queen Mary's Rose Garden

The Parks

Left lying about haphazard and un-filled-in on the grey map of London are the green patches of the parks: big ones like Richmond Park and Hampstead Heath, middle-sized ones like Regent's Park with Primrose Hill, tiny ones like St James's Park and Green Park which, though separate now, used to form one continuous tract with Hyde Park. They are the remains of the grass and woodland tract that once surrounded London, parts later appropriated and protected as royal hunting preserves, parts privately owned, parts (particularly to the south) common land for the people which somehow contrived to avoid being enclosed and built over. All are now well-wooded areas of grass, usually sparkling with ponds or lakes, and criss-crossed by asphalt paths. But in other respects they have plenty of individuality. The Royal Parks are the grandest. St James's Park with its winding lakeside path, its footbridge, fountains and ducks, has some of the informality of a garden. Green Park with its great plane avenue stretching from the Victoria Monument to Piccadilly is more formal, despite its midday sun-bathers. Hyde Park has the same skilfully contrived casualness as a stretch of rural English parkland, an effect heightened by the long shaded rides for horsemen. But just across the dividing roadway, Kensington Gardens with its radiating avenues and its bits of sculpture instantly seems neater. It has shaped trees, clipped hedges, and brown- or red-brick buildings with white stone ornament. Regent's Park is a more recent contrivance, a wholly conscious one by John Nash, who could not only imagine a busy utilitarian canal as a thing of profit *and* beauty but could talk others into seeing it too. Hampstead Heath is truly rural in aspect: despite the encroaching villas that peep through the foliage at its

edges, it still seems like a wilderness, its copses and knolls, muddied ravines and bits of sandy heathland all very much like the backgrounds in a set of sporting prints.

The parks serve as sports-grounds, gardens, adventure-playgrounds, ski- and toboggan-slopes in season, scenery for the surrounding flats, or foils (as in Victoria Park) to industry, deer parks (Richmond Park), car-parks (Epping Forest) and vantage-points from which to survey London itself. The best views of the city are from the slopes of Primrose Hill, Greenwich Park and the Heath. But elsewhere in the parks this heady view of a city lying at one's feet can often become an intrusive and distracting reminder of a world one would rather for a moment forget. As soon as buildings got much taller than plane trees this became impossible; tall blocks now rise above the parkland foliage wherever you look, making the trees seem smaller and meaner. What is more, the parks really *are* getting smaller, shrunken and dog-eared and worn away at the edges. Much of Epping Forest is now roundabout and expressway; a fast internal motor road, impossible to cross, cuts Hyde Park off from Park Lane so that one can only get to it through dark wet tunnels which smell of urine; St James's Park is bounded by a six-lane motorway, with at one end a giant car-park as big as a parade ground (which it occasionally is) and at the other a fast roundabout which a brave pedestrian negotiates at his or her peril.

Yet with all their flaws the parks remain beautiful and restful and relatively un-built-on even in an unscrupulous economic climate in which every square yard is priceless. In a city which stinks of cars they smell of blossom and flowers, mown hay and autumn leaves. They offer an escape, and make London seem fresher and more open.

St James's Park and Whitehall

If you pause on the footbridge across the lake in St James's Park and look east towards Whitehall, you see one of London's finest views, the spires and domes of Whitehall Court and the Horse Guards and the towers of the Foreign Office, across the willows of Duck Island. This view is entirely man-made. Once one would have seen here a swampy field where the St James's Hospital lepers kept their hogs; there was no lake, only marsh which Henry VIII drained. One or two ponds survived, however, and Charles II extended these into a longer strip of water called the Canal, where he enjoyed feeding the ducks and bathing. It was only in 1828 that the Canal was remodelled by Nash into its pleasantly irregular curving shape.

The wildfowl as well as the lake have a long ancestry. Charles II was given two pelicans by the Russian ambassador for the menagerie in Birdcage Walk and there are still pelicans on the lake now. James I's two crocodiles must have died without issue. Charles also planted fruit trees in the park and it then began to take on the agreeably garden-like aspect it still has today. Prettily winding pathways and clumps of shrubbery add to the effect. With diving ducks still easily seen even when they are underwater, geese, pelicans and coots picking their way across the grassy lake margins and handfuls of tame sparrows enjoying the visitors' crumbs, it is all like a splendid aviary without the wires.

St James's Park from the bridge

Green Park: Queen's Walk and Spencer House

Green Park: the Broad Walk

Green Park and the Broad Walk

Green Park is rather more straight-laced than St James's. Its distinctive feature is Broad Walk, a fine avenue laid out rather like the Mall with two lines of planes each side but with grass instead of pink tarmac; the side aisles are at their best as misty brown tunnels in autumn. The nice cast-iron lamp-standards and the park benches that keep disappearing from Regent's Park and Primrose Hill are still to be found here in undiminished numbers – no doubt the Parks people keep the best pieces for the plum sites visible from the Palace.

Queen's Walk at the eastern edge separates the park from a row of extremely grand windows, from the Ritz at the Piccadilly end to Lancaster House on the Mall. The best-looking of the older buildings is Spencer House by Vardy, a magnificent Palladian mansion with lovely sculptured figures and ornament on its pediment, and a pretty grove of planes in front of it in the park. The Park Lane houses must have seemed as close as this to *their* park before the road was widened.

Green Park used to be a place for duellists and highwaymen. But now, on a hot summer's day, it looks more like a beach. Deckchairs come out in force; people bring bathing things, towels and magazines, undressing discreetly and expertly before applying sun-cream; parties of schoolchildren picnic in the ring of planes, and the light clouds reflect up onto the bellies of the jumbos and turn them into big silvery tunny fish. The thump and tootle of a military band playing Lionel Bart wafts up from Buckingham Palace, and to my surprise I feel my feet tingling with some long-forgotten emotion; but it is only the Jubilee line rumbling below.

Hyde Park: Rotten Row

Hyde Park and Rotten Row

Hyde Park is the biggest of the Royal Parks, though nowadays, as one burrows under the traffic to get to it, it is hard to imagine it as a wild place where deer could be hunted. It is much wilder-looking than either of its neighbours Green Park or Kensington Gardens, seeming to belong more to the relaxed and unbuttoned vein of English landscaping than to any French or Dutch models. It looks very beautiful around midsummer when the trees are at their thickest, the grass-heads stand heavy and full, and people seem to sail through it waist-deep. There are often horsemen in Rotten Row and strings of riding-school ponies near the Serpentine, and the Horse Guards ride demurely to or from Knightsbridge Barracks every morning. The legal right of assembly in the park has been recognized since 1872, and has been enjoyed both by the Speakers' Corner orators and by the enormous popular anti-nuclear protest marches of the present day.

Hyde Park: anti-nuclear protesters

Hyde Park and the Serpentine

Hyde Park and the Knightsbridge Barracks

Hyde Park and Kensington Gardens

There are few straight lines in Hyde Park and the main one, Rotten Row, was only cut through by William III so as to get to and from Kensington Palace. But Kensington Gardens are more formal than Hyde Park, laid out with grand avenues of trees which radiate from *ronds-points* marked with obelisks or monuments, or point at some distant landmark like a church spire or (inevitably) Centre Point.

The inconsiderate erection of the Basil Spence Knightsbridge Barracks tower was by far the most harmful event yet suffered by the park: it also seems, in a nuclear age, an oddly exposed place to stack soldiers. It is as inescapable as if the Post Office Tower had been stuck up there. The hotels round Hyde Park Corner (Hilton, Inn on the Park, etc) aren't quite so damaging because they aren't so high. One has only to compare the effect of the plaster terraces of Bayswater along the north of the park, or the Nash terraces round Regent's Park, to realize that buildings can be as big as barracks without necessarily being as brutal.

The romantic ideals of Empire, finely carved in stone, stand at the four corners of the Albert Memorial, but the residual reality of it eddies round their plinths. No roads run through the Gardens, which are therefore quieter, less eroded and more sedate than the park, and are still the haunt of nannies. And even within the protected Gardens are further preserves: the bizarre Italianate water garden at the end of the Long Water, and the gardens of Kensington Palace with the lovely pleached lime alley just south of the Orangery House. This last, a beguiling red-brick building with its arches and its banded rustication, has a familiar handwriting, and so it ought: it was designed for Queen Anne by Hawksmoor, and modified by Vanbrugh. It's difficult to stroll casually away across the park from Kensington Palace: wherever you want to go, you can only get there by a grand avenue.

Kensington Gardens across the Round Pond

Kensington Palace, the Orangery House

Kensington Palace

Kensington Gardens

Henry Moore arch

End of the Long Water

Rotten Row

Vista towards St Mary Abbotts

Albert Memorial

Kensington Palace

The Lake, Regent's Park

Regent's Park

Romantic Regent's Park is even more a conscious creation than orderly Kensington Gardens, and because the original buildings and landscape alike were effectively one man's work, all the scenic effects tend in the same purposeful direction. But Nash, even with all his ingenuity and with the backing of his intimate friend the Prince Regent to whose glory the whole thing was dedicated, could not push through all he wanted. The canal for example flows round the northern perimeter instead of through the central lake; the fifty-six villas and the inner circle of fine houses he envisaged were never realized: there is an unfilled gap between the great terraces. Yet the whole remarkable spectacle is really a Nash invention: above all the long white-painted plaster façades seen through splendid trees or reflected in between the islets of the curving lake. It no longer really matters whether the buildings behind the façades have been ripped out, or what they are now used for; in its essentials Nash's vision has survived.

His intentions did not extend to the detailed execution of the terraces, a job he could not be bothered with and was glad to delegate. The buildings' quality varies with the architect. The grandest of all, Cumberland Terrace, is half dock-scale warehouse, half film-set: the big sculpture-filled pediment is purely, as Wren would have said, 'for pomp', with not even an attic behind it; the columns are there to create light, shade and grandeur, which they do to perfection. The best way to see it is from the front, and quite close-to; from the side the falseness of the pediment is irritating, like a triangular poster hoarding, and from any distance away Nash's façade is now overtopped by the Camden flats of the 1960s.

Despite the ladylike Rose Garden, Regent's Park is not so classy as the other central parks: its benches are filled not by Kensington nannies but by Camden winos and its sportsmen bring footballs, not horses. The beautiful ducks have been dying off in the recent hot dry summers, due to botulism caused by the stagnant water. Herons still nest on the lake islands: their thrown-together nests are landmarks in winter. But the characteristic winter foreground to the Nash stucco is a line of seagulls on a goal-post and the background the minaret and gilded dome of a new mosque.

Cumberland Terrace, Regent's Park

Regent's Canal and the Zoo

The prettiest parkland stretch of the Regent's Canal lies through the Zoo and just beyond, towards Macclesfield (or 'Blow-up') Bridge. It is loveliest in May when the cow-parsley foams about the footpaths and hawthorn scent hangs in the air. One night in 1874 a steam tug with a string of five barges was passing under the bridge when the third barge, *Tilbury*, filled with five tons of gunpowder which the railways sensibly refused to carry, blew up. The bridge was destroyed and the area devastated. The Albany Barracks guards colonel, thinking it must be the work of Fenians, dispatched troops to the canal. Someone who saw it thought it was 'the end of days, the crack of doom' – improbably, at that period at least. The bridge was rebuilt and dangerous loads prohibited. They now go through London by train.

If you can stand the fishy smell, the best way to get really close to the birds in the Snowdon aviary is to sit just outside it near the canal. The nesting seagulls, half screened by greenery, are only a few feet away. At first the broody birds are hostile and fierce, and if it wasn't for the heavy netting they would seem quite dangerous: they look solid enough, even cuddly like stuffed toys, until alarmed, when they open their beaks to scream at you, and you see down into their red throats and realize that inside the smooth skin the birds are as hollow as aeroplanes. But then, as I draw, they relax and doze off, and I feel protective concern when others, keepers or birds, come and disturb them. The sitting bird displays at its mate when it approaches, then they change places, the new one seeming to settle sensually onto the eggs. Their main foes seem to be the prowling deliberate ibises, the skin over their bald heads looking like a tortoise's or, near the curved beaks, a dried banana. It seems a peaceful place because the waterfall noise masks everything else, traffic, barges, planes, even the children, whose silenced scuffles become like mime. With its heavy cables and thick tubing, this early hi-tech structure has always seemed a terribly clumsy and unsympathetically shaped container for the fragile birds. But as the trees inside grow bigger and the foliage denser, they soften the effect and even the big birds can hide in them.

The Regent's Canal and Macclesfield Bridge

The Snowdon Aviary

Primrose Hill

Primrose Hill is a delightful prospect, a clean rounded skyline and a surface dotted with clumps of hawthorn and bigger chestnuts and plane trees which screen off the surrounding terraces and flats. At sixty metres, the hill is not very high; but it is quite steep enough to toboggan down if it snows, when a sparkling Brueghel landscape complete with magpies, leaping dogs and well-muffled children suddenly emerges above the wintry browns and greys of Chalk Farm. It looks lovely too just before the first lush grass of early summer has been mown, when the luxuriance softens the contours, forms thick dark pools of green shade under the hawthorns, and hides the criss-cross asphalt paths as effectively as the winter snow.

Primrose Hill, December

Primrose Hill, June

Parliament Hill and the Heath

The Heath is a much more mysterious place: twice as big as Hyde Park, every walk a climb, and so hummocky that you are always spurred on by wondering what lies over the next rise. Some of the best views of London are those from Parliament Hill, the best thick woodland is at Kenwood, and the Heath's various ponds are the only ones near central London with proper mud and sandy banks instead of asphalt. The Fleet River begins here and indeed you are never very far from water on the Heath; even in summer there are soft and boggy bits where yellow streams trickle through the soil, and shoes get muddier than you expect. The cleanest and prettiest time to see it is on a bright cold day in winter, when the sun warms anyone who keeps moving but cannot thaw out the icy ground, so that one can walk dry-shod on the hard-frozen surface of even the squelchiest bits. Last summer's grass still stands bleached and yellow, deep drifts of dry leaves still lie in sheltered clumps of woodland; blackbirds and thrushes rustle about in their depths; determined joggers and heavy outward-bound jets lumber noisily northwards.

I pass those hollow-trunked and low-spreading trees in which my children like to play; skirt the neat paling at the edge of Kenwood and avoid the cinders of the Vale of Health; and find that, even in bare and open winter, one can arrive at the busy road that crosses the northern edge of the Heath almost before realizing it is there.

The Heath is inevitably threatened by the same pressures as other open spaces. Some are temporary, as when gipsies arrive *en masse* and turn it into a car-park and rubbish dump. But some are permanent: the Hampstead Ponds slopes near where Keats lived are for ever going to be overlooked and made more urban by the big block of the Royal Free Hospital. But we all get ill at some point and need looking after, preferably in a nice place with a view; and if we are to build near an open space, better a hospital for everyone than a barracks. Yet curiously enough that is what the Royal Free, like other hospitals, might turn into: in war-time the treatment of American soldiers would take precedence here over British patients. A large space to bury both has been designated on the Heath not too far away, near the prehistoric grave-mound on Parliament Hill. Who will do the burying is unclear.

London from Parliament Hill

Hollow trees near Kenwood

Hampstead Heath and the Royal Free Hospital

Hampstead Heath near Kenwood

Victoria Park and Peckham Rye

Unlike the Royal Parks which were first
hunting land, then royal gardens, and only
later turned over to public use, Victoria Park
was deliberately created to make life nicer for
the poor and run-down districts around. These
had formerly been leafy landscapes of country
retreats and girls' boarding schools. In 1842
the park was laid out by Nash's son-in-law
James Pennethorne with lakes and fine winding
avenues of planes. Two sides are bounded by
canals, the Regent's Canal and its old offshoot
the short Hertford Canal; beyond this last, the
contrast of the old timber yards and the newish
flats of Old Ford makes a typical East End
landscape. The park has a nice Victorian shelter
and two historic curiosities, the hooded stone
shelters from George Dance's 1758–62
widening of Old London Bridge.

Victoria Park towards Old Ford

Victoria Park: shelter and fountain

Crystal Palace Park dinosaur

Commons had always been *common*, for the public. For some reason south London has a wealth of them, far more than the north, that at Peckham Rye being an isolated reminder of the eighteenth century when all around the village were fields and market gardens. The boy Blake saw angels in an oak tree here, but anyone can see dinosaurs behind the Crystal Palace.

Peckham Rye Common

Epping Forest near Claypit Hill

Epping Forest and Richmond Park

Epping Forest is what remains of the royal hunting ground of the Saxons, Normans and Tudors. Too bumpy to let you see far in any direction, it feels bigger than it is and you quickly get lost, but you cannot for long escape the sound of traffic and you hear the roads long before you see them. At any fine weekend the roads become extended car-parks, yet by wandering a few yards beneath the lovely beeches you can escape into reasonable seclusion and into a world of fallen trees, holly thickets, ponds and little streams; I saw a fox cub sitting nonchalantly at the mouth of its hole. The characteristic shape of the beeches and hornbeams (spreading from a short thick bole and easy for children to climb) is due to pollarding for firewood in the past; luckily for Epping it is no longer worth gathering, as our warmth now comes from older forests.

Richmond Palace has gone but its Old Deer Park remains, grand and open like Turner's Petworth and more expansive than Epping, the rises, plateaux, lowland plains and much-photographed wildlife making me think of Kenya. Near the Ham Gate there is a more typically English scene; a picturesque valley where the road winds between ponds which reflect gnarled oaks like Crome's and Gainsborough's. Overhead a hawk hovers and every minute or two an airliner breaks through the clouds and heads for Heathrow.

Richmond Park from Broomfield Hill

The West End

Long after the City had been built, burnt down and rebuilt, the West End was still mostly fields. This meant that when in the late seventeenth and eighteenth centuries its land-owners began to develop their estates, they could do so in an orderly and considered fashion. Indeed even now you could still draw quite a good plan of it on squared paper, which you certainly couldn't of the City. Many of the tree-filled squares and terraces round which this development took shape are still there, some like Bedford Square with the original three- and four-storey houses intact, some like Berkeley Square almost entirely rebuilt but even so still giving space and structure to the West End scene today.

Of its chief roads, Piccadilly and Oxford Street were ancient highways westwards, the latter of Roman origin. Marylebone Road and Euston Road were laid out from scratch on green fields as part of the New Road of 1757 round north London. But Shaftesbury Avenue and Charing Cross Road, New Oxford Street and Kingsway were all cut through squalid and run-down areas mainly to speed up traffic flow but incidentally to clear some slums, though the first two merely widened existing lanes and streets. The genesis and purpose of Regent Street is much more interesting. It was conceived by John Nash as a magnificent triumphal way between Marylebone Park (now Regent's Park) and Carlton House, the house of his close friend the Prince Regent. Nash's wife had probably been the Prince's mistress and the consequent cash and social position enjoyed by Nash enabled him to push through this and other ambitious plans where mere energy and skill might not have been enough. The road was an essential link if the Regent's Park development was to make a profit. It worked, and though it has taken a beating since, it still does.

One of the advantages Nash promised was some early social engineering; the road would separate the workers and tradesmen to the east from the gentry to the west, for great differences were already emerging within the West End. Though the basic square-and-terrace pattern can still be seen throughout, its different districts have gone on developing in various ways and have acquired great individuality. Rackety showbiz Soho with its Chinese fringe is a far cry from sober and scholarly Bloomsbury, as is cosmopolitan and still slightly bohemian Fitzrovia from

Seifertia and the calculated vulgarities of Oxford Street. The jam-packed video and hi-fi bazaars of Tottenham Court Road are a far remove from the aloof windows and cool interiors of Cork Street or the bright and expensive boutiques of South Molton Street and Covent Garden. Hardly anybody actually *lives* in Soho Square or Berkeley Square nowadays, yet Belgravia with its butlers and chauffeurs is still as rich and residential as ever. And as smart West End shops retreat inexorably westwards, they leave behind a few elegant but crippled survivors amid the touristy remnants of Nash's Piccadilly Circus.

Since people come to the West End for fun as well as to work, it has a lively and expectant air. The fun is on two levels. There is the established and formal kind, of theatres and cinemas and restaurants, and the incidental kind on the pavements: the fruit barrows and flower stalls, the street musicians and jugglers and balloon-sellers. Both add elements of sparkle and excitement which are missing from the more sober and work-oriented City streets. And since this is where the crowds are, the ads are here too: big, impersonal and lit-up on the Piccadilly Circus hoardings, small and pathetic on the Oxford Circus sandwich-board men, squalid on the parking-meters and litter-bins. The street style is changing too. When the weather is warm, the pubs and cafés overflow onto the pavements more freely than they used to, and make them more like those of a continental city. It is nice to sit in the open air in the Covent Garden piazza and watch the crowds drawn there by the new shops and the general stylishness and enjoying the continental square layout first imported by Inigo Jones.

But there is another side to the coin. Fewer and fewer people can afford to live in the West End; interesting-looking old businesses get replaced by boring hotels and offices; gum-strewn Carnaby Street shows what can happen once a new broom wears thin. And in the West End more than elsewhere one feels that London is increasingly being marketed as 'London': a place of quaintly helmeted policemen and cuddly-toy guardsmen, horse-drawn restaurant advertisements, red and blue tube signs and streets whose names sound famous but are not really much to look at. If the myth begins to look too hollow or too cynical, the shabby old West End will have a lot of catching up to do.

Piccadilly circus

West End street traders

There were street traders or costermongers long before there were any shopkeepers. After that, they went on selling to people too poor to buy much at once or too shabby to be let into shops, this last now a dwindling category. The traders, never very popular with the authorities and sometimes illegal, avoided licensing restrictions only by keeping on the move, pushing their heavy three-quarter-ton barrows up to ten miles in a day; and even though they now work mainly from fixed pitches, most are still barrow-based, trundling into place each morning and away again at night.

Some of the street traders still have strong Victorian or Edwardian overtones, like the chestnut man, the bell-ringing rag-and-bone man and the horse-drawn any-old-iron man with his mattresses and old armchairs. Pegg's eels, shrimps and cockles stall near Cambridge Circus is a reminder of a more distant time when wet fish were as freely sold on the pavement as fruit or flowers are now. These last make the prettiest barrows, their stock changing key with the season, but always nice to look at and well-set-out. Nothing else ever looks as good as the real thing simply displayed, and here it is.

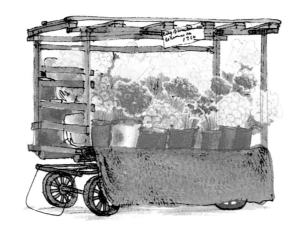

But not everyone who works on the pavement is a freelance. Mayhew's crossing sweepers are council employees now; the popcorn lady sells Playtime Popcorn ('it's fun to eat') for Trusthouse Forte; the motor-cycle messenger works on his own bike, but delivers for an agency. The miniature reproduction horse-bus advertises something (in this case a pub), like most of the horse-drawn carriages or vans in the West End streets today.

Home-made ballad sheets and playbills, like the running patterers who related the news, have long ago been driven off the streets by magazines and newspapers. But home-made advice may still be had for elevenpence from the sensible 'Less Lust from Less Protein' man who walks the pavements near Oxford Circus. He also recommends Less Sitting, and practises what he preaches.

Many of these very durable flower and vegetable barrows bear the name Ellen Keeley incised in good cursive script on their wooden wheels and spars; her barrows have become an evocative symbol of a vanishing London. Other familiar West End symbols like London Transport roundels and familiar street names adorn the many pavement souvenir stalls, along with toy guardsmen and cardboard policemen's helmets. 'Souvenir' has lately become a dirty word associated only with ephemeral rubbish, and for good reason. This is a pity: Sunderland jugs, Staffordshire figures and many other beautiful objects in our homes and museums were originally bought quite cheaply as souvenirs. London could do with some better ones.

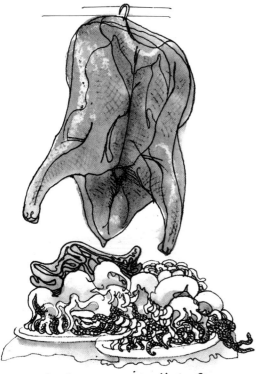

Duck and squid, Lisle Street

Dragon, Gerrard Street

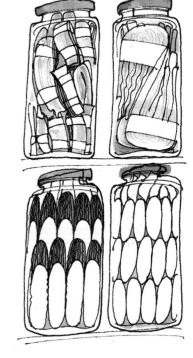

Roots, Lisle Street

George II, Golden Square

Restaurant uniforms, Dean Street

Chinese couple, Gerrard Street

Soho

'Soho!' meant 'tally-ho!' – it was in the sixteenth century an area given over to the chase, as in a way it still is: an exotic quarter of strip joints, sex cinemas and shops and 'adult' clubs. But this, like the strong Chinese and Bengali element, is a fairly recent aspect of Soho, which for long was merely respectably cosmopolitan; indeed, it actually started off extremely grandly, with the laying-out of Golden Square in 1673 and Soho Square in

1681, for aristocrats to occupy. But within a few years, industrious French Protestant refugees were arriving to establish Soho as London's main foreign quarter; its central pub is nicknamed 'The French'. In the eighteenth century it was literary, artistic and bohemian; in the nineteenth it became extremely overcrowded, unhealthy, theatrical and tarty. But it was only early this century that it became well-known for good restaurants, and it is the influx of successive waves of Greek, French, German, Italian, Chinese and Bengali

waiters, chefs and restaurateurs that has kept it cosmopolitan today. Their pots and pans and waiters' clothes can be got in Old Compton Street just round the corner from the French pâtisserie. The Chinese are in Gerrard and Lisle Streets, the ground-floor windows of their sober Georgian houses full of jars of strange sliced roots, varnished ducks, Chinese hotel ware and dragons. Soho's central landmark – appropriately bizarre yet elegant – is the tower of St Anne's Church, which now has diners' cars for a congregation.

St Anne, Soho

24-28 Greek Street

British Library

The British Museum and Gower St

Bloomsbury comprises the Bedford estate north of New Oxford Street. Its spinal cord is Gower Street which connects its dominating features, the British Museum and Library in the south and University College in the north, both in the radical pagan classical style, unlike the establishment Christian gothic of Westminster. The two are separated by the sixty-metre-high tower of Senate House, an undervalued thirties building which commanded the skies of the district until the clumsy Post Offce Tower gatecrashed in. I planned at first to draw Sir Robert Smirke's fine Ionic colonnade and portico to the museum, but changed to his brother Sydney's great blue-domed library, looking like an inside-out eggshell, as soon as I saw it. Near the other end of Gower Street, University College – which was to free higher education from its male Anglican yoke and let in Jews, Catholics and ultimately even women – is disappointing architecturally, but its Hospital by Alfred (Pru) Waterhouse is a romantic building with a curious X-shaped ground-plan and a sharply cut jagged skyline.

Senate House, London University

University College Hospital

Red Lion, Duke of York Street

West End pubs

Much of the style of the West End scene comes from its multitudinous pubs. They come in many sizes and qualities, but externally at least they all have something in common: they all have to cry their wares, to make themselves known. So pub fronts have to be architectural posters. Besides displaying the name clearly, they have to look welcoming, solid, convivial and even a bit florid, and generally as old as possible: a new pub is about as attractive as a new church. Restraint, as in the Coach and Horses which is simply a minimally adapted house-front, and refinement, as in the elegant *art nouveau* Rising Sun, are unusual. But a touch of the theatre is general: the Cross Keys looks like an Inigo Jones masque design, and the boisterous gilt figures and decoration on the flamboyant Salisbury would go very well on a Victorian merry-go-round.

Once inside, the people in a pub matter almost as much as its looks, but not quite. The prettiest interior I know is the Red Lion's in Duke of York Street, off St James's Square. It sparkles with cut and bevelled glass and engraved mirrors and is enlivened by the gleaming curves of its polished mahogany and the glimpses you get through the arches into the other bar. It is busy at lunchtime and with all its fine glass it looks dangerously fragile for its purpose, but it has clearly survived quite undamaged, even by the offers of rich visitors who would have liked the mirrors. It remains, well-made, durable and resplendent, the perfect Victorian pub.

Lamb and Flag, Rose Street

Cross Keys, Endell Street

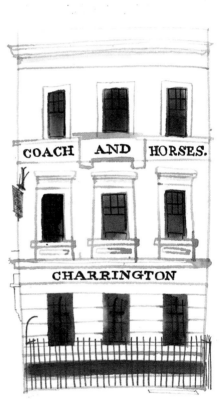

Coach and Horses, Hill Street

Rising Sun,
Tottenham Court Road

Sun Tavern, Long Acre

The Salisbury, St Martin's Lane

Red Lion, Duke of York Street

West End theatres

Theatres also, like pubs but even more like churches, have to advertise their presence, look grand, be landmarks. Traditionally they have used the same devices as churches, though on different scales: grand entrances, imposing columns, plaster and ironwork, statuary, big (if mortal) names, bold lettering. The Coliseum even has a steeple too, just like St Martin-in-the-Fields (the one on the right). They also try to get a good position: the finest vista from St James's Square is the one closed by the distant Corinthian portico of John Nash's Theatre Royal, Haymarket, to which he gave an important position overlooking Regent Street.

The grandeur may be applied without much ceremony or even as an afterthought, like the porch and colonnade which a later architect tacked onto Wyatt's austere brick-box Theatre Royal in Drury Lane. But there are no afterthoughts about the enormous curving cliff-like front of the Palace Theatre, built as D'Oyly Carte's Opera House and now Andrew Lloyd Webber's.

The Coliseum, St Martin's Lane and St Martin-in-the-Fields

Theatre Royal, Haymarket

Theatre Royal, Drury Lane

The Palace Theatre, Cambridge Circus

Floral Hall and the Royal Opera House

Opera House and street theatre

There was nothing grand, however, about the siting of the Royal Opera House among the potatoes, printers and policemen of Covent Garden. The architect Edward Barry coped equally well with the Opera House and the humbler Floral Hall next door. The interior of the first is most beautiful; its rear has recently been elegantly and tactfully extended in the original style towards the market. Though camped-up a bit, the decorative conventions of comic opera live on in nearby Neal's Yard. But outside in the actual world, real street theatre – intended or not – flourishes on every hand.

Neal's Yard

London Street Theatre

Covent Garden: the Piazza

Two points of view exist about the new Covent Garden. One is admiration for the energy, care and style with which part at any rate of a most historic district has been cleared out, restored and re-animated. The other is regret that the genuine interest of an ancient working quarter has vanished as London's oldest square, its market and its surroundings have been turned into a tourist paradise, a profitable but expensive Eliza Doolittle theme-park. This was precisely the original idea of the long-discredited development plan of 1968, which cynically described the NE–SW axis running through the market as a 'character route', between the new hotels and offices; and it is pretty much what has come to pass.

The piazza was built by Inigo Jones for the fourth Earl of Bedford in 1631–8; the Italian-inspired arcades originally ran right along the north side, gardens opened to the south. A market was established in the middle quite soon, in 1721, but was only housed in Fowler's excellent buildings in 1828–31. The vistas along King Street and Henrietta Street are fine, St Paul, Covent Garden (hidden here beyond the market buildings) looks lovely, and enough of Inigo Jones's concept remains for one to marvel at his vision.

Covent Garden, the piazza

Tottenham Court Road and Fitzrovia

Seifert Circus is the hub and symbol of the new, scruffier West End. The fussy yet cumbersome faceted patterning of the concrete walling rises high above the shoddy and inaccessible fountains of an 'ornamental' pool at its base, amid hoardings, tub-planted saplings and clogged traffic. Temporarily shored-up ends of terraces back onto it; equally impermanent-looking single-storey video, hi-fi and sex shops stretch up Tottenham Court Road from it as far as the old Heal's building recently revamped by Conran. To the west is Fitzrovia. Its grandest monument, Robert Adam's Fitzroy Square, would sit well in Bath or Edinburgh, but the square's fine plane trees are now edged by pedestrianized streets made unwelcoming by graceless street furniture, cracked paving-stones and anti-traffic gullies: the unity of façades, pavements, railings and stone setts that distinguish Bath have here been ignorantly destroyed. The Adam façades are a lasting monument to better sense.

Centre Point and St Giles-in-the-fields

Tottenham Court Road, west side

Fitzroy Square, west side

131

132

Euston Road

Tottenham Court Road peters out at the top
end in a mish-mash of 'traffic engineering'.
Across Euston Road stands a striking example
of a lately arrived phenomenon: the oddly
contrasting aspects of the sky to the north,
south, east and west can all be taken in at a
single glance as they are reflected off the walls
of the offices opposite. The mirror panels belly
out or curve in more than can have been
intended, causing quaint distortions which
recall the work of the early glaziers more than
the precision of hi-tech.

Euston Road

The railway stations

The main railway lines from the north all end up along the Euston Road, the present name for a section of the New Road built to connect Paddington to the City through the fields north of London: the first by-pass ever built. The termini stand quite close together in inverse degrees of magnificence: the less used, the more splendid. Sir George Gilbert Scott's hotel of 1868–74 which formed a buffer for the Midland Railway provides one of London's most romantic skylines, much of it rich and dark still in its currently half-cleaned state. It is all spire and stripy pinnacles and finicky but scholarly gothic detail, with Britannia sensibly surveying the world not from the top but from only about halfway up. The best view of both St Pancras and Cubitt's earlier King's Cross (1850) is from across the Euston Road; the King's Cross hotel is placed to the side, so that one has a clear view of at least the upper part of Cubitt's stock-brick train-sheds, the arrival and departure sides firmly separated by a big plain clock-tower. The foreground of each station is dull and shoddy, St Pancras by neglect and King's Cross by design, inexcusably, by British Rail's own team of architects.

There is more of the same half a mile up the road at Euston, where Philip Hardwick's monumental Arch was needlessly demolished in 1961 so that the platforms could be lengthened; they never were. All that remains are the two flanking pavilions, with their arbitrary and slightly poignant lists of once-important towns on the London, Midland and Scottish. Seifert's new (1980) railway offices gleam blackly over them. The only relatively unchanged station forecourt is further west still at Marylebone, where cast- and wrought-iron canopies still shelter a few commuters. It is London's last and smallest terminus, built in 1898–9. Like all the other façades it gives dignified architectural expression to the arrival of people into a great city: contrast the central underground stations today.

St Pancras Station

Marylebone Station

Euston Station

King's Cross Station

All Souls, Langham Place and the BBC

Langham Place and Camden Lock

When John Nash was planning Regent Street, he had to get round two awkward bends. At one, a curve of ninety degrees just north-west of Piccadilly Circus, he built the now vanished Quadrant; at the other, a dog's-leg just north of Oxford Circus, he put the handsome church of All Souls, Langham Place. It still looks well, but its undisputed command of the scene disappeared in 1931 when the BBC built Broadcasting House behind and above it. However, the two don't look bad together, sharing the same curves and even in some ways the same securely established standards and aspirations. Eric Gill's fine sculpture of Prospero and Ariel over the main doors suggests decently and credibly the BBC's early idealism, little the worse for its Auntie-ish overtones. The reason for Nash's dog's-leg was that he could not damage the protected view up Portland Place from where the Langham Hotel now stands and where Norman Foster's new BBC soon will. Perhaps it will re-assert the same imaginative values.

But the media have dragged or chased each other a long way down-market since the days of Reith. The architectural expression of this appears in the TV-am studio up the road at Camden Lock, in a building much written-up when it was new. By 1983 Gill sculptures had given way to a dozen fibreglass boiled eggs: an exchange all too appropriate to a business in which people's attention and responses have to be bought and sold like groceries, a business with more tarts than Aunties.

TV·am studio, Camden Lock

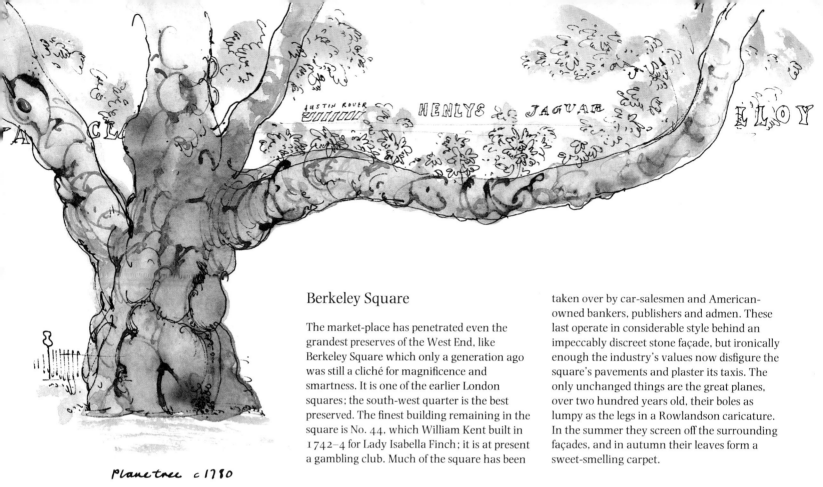

Berkeley Square

The market-place has penetrated even the grandest preserves of the West End, like Berkeley Square which only a generation ago was still a cliché for magnificence and smartness. It is one of the earlier London squares; the south-west quarter is the best preserved. The finest building remaining in the square is No. 44, which William Kent built in 1742–4 for Lady Isabella Finch; it is at present a gambling club. Much of the square has been taken over by car-salesmen and American-owned bankers, publishers and admen. These last operate in considerable style behind an impeccably discreet stone façade, but ironically enough the industry's values now disfigure the square's pavements and plaster its taxis. The only unchanged things are the great planes, over two hundred years old, their boles as lumpy as the legs in a Rowlandson caricature. In the summer they screen off the surrounding façades, and in autumn their leaves form a sweet-smelling carpet.

Plane tree c 1780

J. Walter Thompson advertising agency

44 Berkeley Square

Mayfair and Grosvenor Square

South Molton Street is a pedestrian area that really works: a pleasantly animated place to stroll up and down looking at lively windows full of clothes, or just to sit and have a coffee or a beer. The pavement belongs to people, not cars. At the southern end, where it joins Brook Street, the Tyburn (burn = stream) used to flow, giving Brook Street its name, before going underground into Conduit Street and eventually reaching the City as drinking water.

South Molton Street is mostly of brick and painted plaster, like the pretty Grosvenor Chapel on South Audley Street built in 1739 as part of the new Grosvenor Square development; the chapel backs onto a delightful but less formal patch of greenery, St George's Gardens. But much of the Mayfair building is of rose-coloured terracotta, a material that encouraged a wealth of detailing that can seem either splendidly inventive or just plain fussy. I like the Mount Street façades for their Dutch fretwork skyline and the recesses or holes punched through them as carelessly as if they were part of a stage set. There is a nice-looking game shop lower down opposite the Connaught Hotel, and round the corner at the bottom of Davies Street one can see, through an archway into an antique dealer's yard, a surprising three-headed lady: part pig, part dog, part cow. There is something almost as unexpected up the road, off Duke Street: an electricity sub-station made the pretext for a raised and pavilioned piazza, sunlit above the traffic.

Just south of this is a far bigger area of greenery and relative peace. Grosvenor Square was the core of the development by Sir Richard Grosvenor, from about 1720, that turned the northern of his two great estates from farmland into what is now Mayfair. In the other estate, now Belgravia, building only began over a century later. Grosvenor Square is the largest of the London squares, and it used to be the grandest. But the expense of buying a lease there, and the prospect of renewing it at a higher price, and keeping up an enormous house, meant that only the very richest could live there; and though they were willing to employ good architects, they would not tolerate the imposition of any architectural unity.

When after the first war the rest of Mayfair began to fill with offices and car showrooms and ad agencies, Grosvenor Square abandoned itself lock stock and barrel to the special relationship with the United States. Hardly any of its old buildings have survived; most of the square is now offices and hotels in would-be neo-American-colonial style, but the west side consists of the US Embassy of 1958–61, a surprisingly undistinguished building for its architect Saarinen: a dull box trivialized by aluminium-gilt trim, and surmounted by a large bronze eagle, tactlessly hawkish in style.

140

South Molton Street

Davies Street courtyard

Mount Street poultry and game

Piazza off Duke Street

Grosvenor Chapel

Mount Street, south side

US Embassy, Grosvenor Square

95-99 Park Lane

Park Lane

Hemmed in by Lutyens-faced hotels, offices, and
car showrooms, a few remnants of Georgian
Park Lane can still be seen, including Disraeli's
old house, No. 93, on the left of the drawing.
The bow windows and fine cast-iron verandahs
of these Park Lane houses had an almost
uninterrupted view of Hyde Park. But in 1961
the park was moved fifty yards further west,
and now these windows look out onto their
own jam-packed parking-lot and eight lanes of
traffic separated by a crudely barricaded grass
patch. It is impossible to cross the further
northerly flow of fast traffic, which belts up to
Marble Arch unimpeded by lights; you can only
get to the park by using the widely separated
and smelly subways. One might as well stroll
up the M1.

Hyde Park from Brook Gate

Hyde Park Corner

To anyone coming from the west, the country used to end and the town to begin at the Hyde Park Corner turnpike, so that Wellington had reason as well as nerve to call Apsley House 'Number One, London'. No one could do so now, for it is utterly isolated by traffic: a good house in a rotten position. There are compensations: the roundabout facing it and surrounding the Wellington Arch is so enormous that from the middle of it the actual flow of traffic seems quite distant. Sitting there in the sun is quiet and peaceful, and one can draw undisturbed since the place is now fairly inaccessible – it is less trouble to stay underground as you cross the road than to surface in the middle. But these are meagre rewards for the despoliation of one of London's most important places.

Until 1883, Decimus Burton's Wellington Arch stood opposite his delicate Ionic screen into Hyde Park and formed the northern gate to Buckingham Palace gardens. but then it was moved to its present position facing Constitution Hill, and it now provides a triumphal arch through which a troop of Household Cavalry ride every morning for the Changing of the Guard. The pageantry always makes a romantic sight. This spirit is echoed in the fine bronze sculptured soldiers who stand guard round Wellington mounted on his horse, Copenhagen, in front of his old house. A much bigger version of the same subject used to stand on top of the Wellington Arch, but it was replaced by Peace and the Quadriga much as one seagull dislodges another from the top of a mast. Despite the ticklish subject this adds a flourish to a flat skyline and still looks highly effective as a bit of sculpture.

Hyde Park Corner and Apsley House

The Food Halls at Harrods

West End shops

Most of the West End's well-stocked and presentable shops are interesting more for what they sell than for what they are. But hidden away among them are others which are historically or graphically interesting even if, like Fribourg and Treyer in the Haymarket, they happen currently to have ground to a halt. This very elegant shop-front of *c.* 1770, dusty and shuttered at present, was itself an addition to a slightly older house. Shop and house, however, remain well-knit; indeed, the shop windows still look quite domestic. Paxton and Whitfield could only be a shop: the display area of the window is getting bigger and the lettering

above it more emphatic. The formula is repeated in Cornelissen, the artists' colour-men in Great Queen Street, in whose windows early advertising material (coats of arms, prize medals and the like) is now beginning to compete with the skilful display of the goods. Where these do not look very interesting, the display and the typography naturally count for more: James Smith and Son, *c.* 1880, is a monument to the skill and imagination of the late-Victorian signwriter and gilder in adding lustre and romance to the humble umbrella. The idea of suggesting extreme grandeur by majestic understatement, as employed by Sotheby's, has yet to catch on. Its opposite, splendour by association, reaches its climax in

Harrods' finely tiled Food Halls, *c.* 1905, a magnificent achievement and much more interesting than its exterior. Harrods really only works outside when the electric light bulbs turn it into the Brompton Road Blackpool Illuminations. Gordon Selfridge must have sensed this danger when he commissioned 'The Queen of Time' as a necessary focal point for his equally long frontage on Oxford Street. At about the same time, Michelin was ebulliently putting car tyres into the architecture where Britons would have put classical capitals. Nowadays, architects meekly leave this sort of inventiveness to the display experts, or like Souvenirs of London dispense with the shop-front altogether.

Haymarket

Jermyn Street

Great Queen Street

New Oxford Street

Oxford Street

Oxford Street

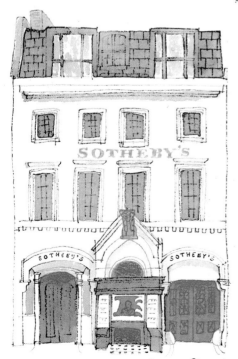

New Bond Street

Brompton Road

Fulham Road

Belgravia and Sloane Square

At the north corner of Belgrave Square Wilton and Grosvenor Crescents meet in a dizzily swirling landscape of painted stucco. Money is obviously around; in this region of freshly waxed limousines, grey-uniformed chauffeurs and stripy-waistcoated butlers, even the mews are grand. It wasn't always so. Belgravia stands on old market gardens and marsh, which had to be raised with the earth Cubitt dug out of St Katharine's Dock. The London end of the King's Road begins here, running smoothly and magnificently through Eaton Square before changing down for the curve round Peter Jones at Sloane Square. This is one of London's first 'modern' buildings, and its curving curtain wall still looks elegant and sensible.

Wilton Crescent and Grosvenor Crescent

Eccleston Mews

Sloane Square and Peter Jones

South Kensington

Fossils of many kinds are to be found in South Kensington, industrial, architectural and imperial as well as archaeological. The architectural ones by Aston Webb, Waterhouse and others house the museum collections, happily enough in Natural History but with more difficulty in Science where the need to find room for new technology causes evident overcrowding. Artefacts fossilize much quicker than they did in the past, and in the Darwinian struggle for survival the weaker exhibits naturally go under; there used for example to be a lot more beam engines than there are now, all of them wheezing, clanking and grinding ponderously away from time to time. Boulton and Watts's 'Old Bess' of 1777 must be one of the fittest.

Up the road between the Albert Memorial and the square tower of the Imperial Institute sits the Albert Hall, a squat and domed oval building of red brick and terracotta. It was originally to have been designed by Gilbert Scott, who built the memorial, but after various hitches it was eventually built by a couple of soldiers, a Captain Fowke and a Colonel Darracott Scott. Not surprisingly, the influences are somewhat undigested – the Dresden Opera House with traces of the Colosseum. It was to have been called simply the 'Hall of Arts and Sciences', but when she laid the foundation stone Queen Victoria unilaterally christened it the 'Royal Albert'. Its nether regions are enfolded by the rosy and ample curves of Albert Court and Norman Shaw's Albert Hall Mansions. This was London's first-ever block of flats: a splendid affair with fine entrances and a well-provided internal street, and separated from Albert Court by a winding external canyon. It is fitting that the enquiring and scientific but home-loving Albert's name should finally be left clinging not just to his grandiloquent Memorial but also to these practical monuments to music and domestic comfort.

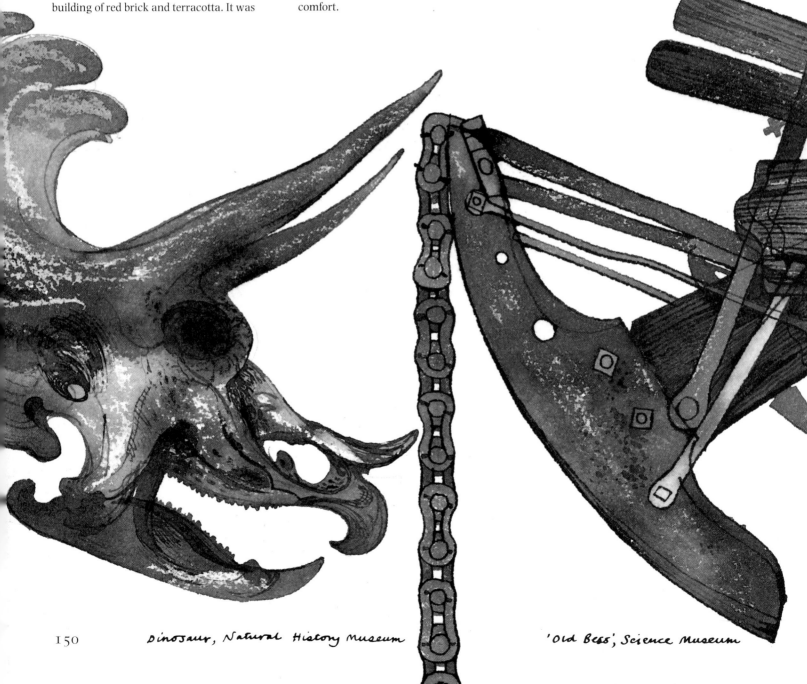

150   Dinosaur, Natural History Museum   'Old Bess', Science Museum

Albert Hall Mansions, the Albert Hall and Albert Court

Villages and Suburbs

London has always been getting bigger, spreading like a blob of treacle wherever it could, and resisting all attempts to contain it. At first the spread was merely into the fields just outside the walls, Spitalfields, Moorfields, Lincoln's Inn Fields and so on; but in due course it engulfed independent communities, villages and hamlets like Islington and Paddington, rivers like the Westbourne and the Tyburn, the Holebourne and the Wandle, cottages and farms, inns and manors, great houses and monastic institutions. Many of these places have simply been swamped – pulled down and built over long ago. Others like Hampstead and Dulwich have come through with some of their own individuality intact. Some isolated buildings like Fenton House and Ham House have survived almost as though time had stood still. But all around, the growth of London has in its turn brought into being regions whose own history is by now every bit as real and interesting as that of the places that were there before.

At first these outlying regions were important and necessary to London. Shoreditch made its furniture, Chelsea threw its pots, Spitalfields wove its silks, Battersea grew its vegetables, Wandsworth Huguenots made its hats. Later they became more important as its bedrooms: one by one, Clapham and New Cross, Tottenham and Wembley, Ruislip and Orpington became places you went home to after work. It is hard to put a collective name to these regions: 'villages', even when it applies, sounds nostalgic, sentimental and pretentious; 'suburban' has long been for many a put-down evoking boring obscurity. But Keats lived in a brand-new semi-detached house in a suburb; and so do many Londoners today.

The earliest surviving architecture is of village streets like Church Row, Hampstead and substantial houses like Vanbrugh's at Greenwich; almost everything smaller has disappeared. Then in the eighteenth and nineteenth centuries brick terrace housing began to spread along the bigger roads out of London. It was an adaptable form: its development can be traced with interest whenever one is stuck in a traffic jam at the Angel or Camberwell, in Clapham High Street or along the Seven Sisters Road. Terrace building is cheaper than detached, and the money saved could go into modest decoration such as door

fanlights (nothing likely to be inflammable had been allowed anyway since the Fire) and into large gardens front and back. Such gardens survive, much the worse for wear, at the top of Pentonville Road. But sooner or later the ground floors of many of these houses became shops or businesses. Cheaply built single-storey top-lit shops were plonked where the nice gardens had been, forming a new low terrace façade which pretty well obscured the original stock-brick terrace far behind; they occasionally survived as a going concern even when the terrace had fallen to bits. Later suburban developments – the long low Victorian terrace house, the pre-1914 villas and the pre-1939 semi-detached ribbons, and the great uniform acreage post-1950 of low red-brick buildings and high concrete ones – have had no such need to adapt to circumstances. They look pretty much the same now as when they were built, just like the railways, whose cheap workmen's tickets brought much of suburbia into being.

The things that *have* had to adapt are the roads, which now have to serve as speedways and car-parks, often both at once. Indeed, parking has altered the appearance of the suburban street far more than anything else. A line of tightly packed cars is now just as much a part of every street as the houses, the pavements and the front walls; more so in fact, since front walls have been knocked down and courtyards and pavements have vanished as people turn their own once-private front gardens into asphalt car-stands. The big optimistic roads of the 1930s have had to be widened, through gardens and houses if need be; only the M4 and Westway and the Brent Cross flyover sail calm and unruffled over the rooftops. The scene under this last is a strange one: in August, mingling with the exhaust fumes you can smell the confined River Brent like a Mediterranean drain; the ducks have vanished and something hard, thick and evil-looking is growing from beneath the drainage holes. Dangerous-sounding traffic honks in rage, and other still bigger cars fill the poster hoardings. Yet there is another suburban smell, of late summer plants; bindweed softens the harsh lines of the concrete posts carrying the netting and barbed wire; the new fencing is already rotting and you can step through to get at the ripe blackberries.

Plough Road, Wandsworth

Dulwich, Greenwich and Blackheath

Remnants of pre-suburban countryside survive on London's outskirts in a few isolated pockets, by dint of good luck and careful preservation. In one or two places, such as Dulwich, a stranger might easily think he or she had suddenly reached the real country, especially in summer when the hedges are thick. Suburban front gardens give way to weathered fencing and gates to stiles, and the smell of elderblossom hangs in the air. It is of course only half rural: the meadows are cricket pitches, the barns pavilions, the villagers only city gents in white flannels. Dulwich has another wholly delightful foretaste of Kentish weather-boarding in Pond Cottages, and also a millpond with brown and white geese and hot tired pigeons lying flopped-out on the grass; but there is so much wire-netting round it that the carefree rural effect looks a bit over-cherished.

Whatever we might think of them now, the carpenters who built Pond Cottages can hardly have thought them picturesque; they were simply plain practical houses. On the other hand, when in the 1720s Sir John Vanbrugh built himself a battlemented and turreted sham castle at Greenwich, he can hardly have thought it anything else. The notion of the picturesque as a fantastic assemblage of more or less authentic architectural details in order to create a consciously romantic effect had not yet been articulated; yet here it is, actually taking shape. Such romanticism draws extra strength from happy accidents, and here fate duly supplied an appropriately blasted-looking oak to frame Vanbrugh's towers. But fate is perverse; where Vanbrugh once looked from his towers down over the Thames towards his fine military buildings at Woolwich Arsenal, there is now a landscape of gasometers and power-station chimneys like batteries of cannon. He would probably have liked it.

The picturesque tradition was in due course seized on and developed by John Nash. But it was felt also, in many more subdued and anonymous instances, as a way of adding interest and appeal to many houses which would otherwise be quite ordinary. The villas along Prince of Wales Road at the edge of Blackheath, less than half a mile from Vanbrugh's castle, are a pretty example, where the inspired addition of a few pediments, some pilasters and some coloured icing turns plain brick boxes into pleasant bits of scenery.

Cricket pitch, Dulwich

Pond Cottages, Dulwich

Vanbrugh Castle, Maze Hill, Greenwich

Villas on Prince of Wales Road, Blackheath

Ham House

Chiswick House

Ham, Chiswick and Hampstead

As London spread, the big houses round it fared better than the defenceless village streets: many have survived, like giant redwoods after a forest fire. They now fulfil a double role, as interesting buildings in their own right but also as useful foils, providing a pause and a change of scale in the brick-and-tile landscapes that surround them. To do this they do not need to be particularly big – Fenton House is not – but big and conspicuous ones are less likely to founder unnoticed. Ham House and Fenton House are seventeenth-century brick-and-no-nonsense – or not much. The busts and the stone quoins on the one, and the wooden balustrade and the two pillars on the other, are the only things that could be called decorative. Everything else is plain, home-grown, straightforward and first-rate. By contrast, Chiswick and Kenwood are eighteenth-century stone and stucco and classically inspired; everything you can see – proportions, details, heavy rustication, delicate Adam ornament – is there primarily to be looked at and admired. But so nowadays are the houses themselves – the price of their survival has been transformation into museums, with only an occasional reminder that they used to be lived in by people. Museum status means a tidy uniformity – postcards, polished floors, trim lawns – which they can never have had as houses.

Fenton House

Kenwood House

The Hurlingham Club

Hurlingham and Putney

Hurlingham House, however, is not open to the public. It stands white and spectacular, like a snowman after a thaw, amid the long Victorian terraces of Fulham and Parsons Green and the oil tanks of Wandsworth. Polo, which was invented here, is no longer played, the pitches having been pinched by the LCC; but croquet goes on in front of the portico as if on a Victorian lawn painted by the Daniells. With its magnificent trees, smooth turf and striped tents it looks like a picture of a medieval tournament. It is a curious yet strangely beautiful anachronism.

Most of the late-nineteenth-century houses in the districts which had been opened up by the railways were built in terraces, but the more substantial of them were individual or semi-detached villas. The most conspicuous and once-splendid of these stand along the bigger roads, often suffering from planning blight and picturesque decay in an acute form, crumbling away behind ivy-covered garden walls and heavy wooden carriage gates that have proved too expensive to keep in good repair. There are some good examples on Haverstock Hill in Hampstead, and others along many of the older roads out of London.

But of all the late-Victorian and Edwardian villas, the nicest to live in are those which look out in front onto quiet, leafy streets and behind onto a pleasant garden landscape where everyone tends their own greenery but enjoys the benefit of everyone else's as well. Such surroundings combine the open pleasures of the country with a relatively easy journey to central London: a seductive enough recipe, but one which hinges on later development being held in reasonable check and not allowed to over-reach itself. A good example is Putney, a riverside town for long appreciated by the well-off but remote enough from London to remain undeveloped until 1880, when the District Line arrived just over the river and the bridge tolls were lifted. Most of Putney's often handsome houses were built between then and the Great War, which gives a pleasantly uniform late-Victorian and Edwardian flavour to the place; little building since then has occurred to spoil it. It is the ideal suburb.

House off Putney Hill

Church Row and Downshire Hill

The nicest-looking row of eighteenth-century village houses is in Church Row, Hampstead. Though they are not a completely unified terrace like Queen Anne's Gate, all were built at the same time (the 1720s) when the recently discovered spring waters made Hampstead important. The brown-brick houses are plonked straight onto the pavement, unprotected save by iron railings. But a century later, when Hampstead was spreading downhill towards advancing London, the new houses were built separated or in pairs and set back off the road behind gardens, hidden by trees and doubly clothed by stucco and creeper. Downshire Hill is still a pretty area, of houses by now unrelated architecturally except in their generally romantic spirit, and provided in 1823 with a suitably picturesque proprietary chapel, also in white stucco, with a wooden bell-tower. St John, Downshire Hill is as pretty inside as out, with its box pews and gallery and general clean airiness. Keats lived nearby in a typically leafy suburban villa. Prints on its walls show how rural Hampstead still looked at that time, with pasturage and farmland and London visible far away in the distance. The furniture and the poet's mementos and the basement kitchen keep alive the warm feeling of human habitation that has escaped altogether from the grander houses, and the garden is tended in the same spirit.

Keats House, Keats Grove, Hampstead

Church Row, Hampstead

House on Downshire Hill, Hampstead

St John's Chapel, Downshire Hill

Downshire Hill, Hampstead

The history of the terrace

After the all-brick Georgian terrace and the all-stucco Regency villa came the half-of-each hybrid that established itself as the standard London Victorian terrace: good yellow stock-brick above and painted stucco below, with occasional excursions upwards by way of pilasters and pediments. So similar are the variants on this model that you can fit a few bays from Belgravia onto a few from Islington and hardly tell them apart; in comparing Caroline Terrace with Gibson Square the only significant differences are the latter's arched windows and doors and its stucco window-surrounds. The stucco was originally invented as a cheaper stone substitute with a matt surface, and though it now glistens and reflects almost like glass when newly painted, it wasn't originally meant to.

The terrace was not as inviolable as it looked. Terraced houses were easily turned into shops once a district began going slightly downhill. Unlike Church Row but like Downshire Hill, the later brick terraced houses strung along the wider roads into London such as Pentonville Road often started off with large gardens in front of them. But later in the nineteenth century this space grew too valuable to leave as it was, and rows of cheaply run-up single-storey shops replaced the gardens, so that now in Camden High Street one can hardly see the original terrace tucked far away behind.

There are similar instances of this process along all the old main roads through the inner suburbs on both sides of the river. Where the street or the district was prosperous enough, the original terraces were eventually rebuilt along with their ground-floor projections, which in the last few decades had become supermarkets or high-street chain-stores. But where the area was really run down, or its fate uncertain because of redevelopment, the terraces simply crumbled away entirely, leaving only the line of shops. Hampstead Road is a specially vivid example of their melancholy and inexorable decline.

Pentonville Road near the Angel, Islington

Camden High Street near Mornington Crescent

Caroline Terrace, Belgravia

Gibson Square, Islington

Hackney Road, Haggerston

Hampstead Road near Euston

Camden Town markets

There are two kinds of markets in Camden Town. The weekends-only kind at Camden Lock, which caters mainly for visitors from elsewhere, has a rather amateurish air, as of people doing it for fun, enjoying each other's company and the pleasure of having something to do. You can find as wide a range of things as you would in a Parisian flea-market; stripped-pine furniture, zebra skins, sheet-music and old clothes and so on. The other kind of market is held daily in Inverness Street and is highly professional. It serves the neighbourhood and a bit beyond with necessities like fruit, veg and flowers, and also with such modest present-day

luxuries as incense, old hand-tools, cats' meat and good cheeses. The traders and the back-up services like street-cleaners and barrow-trundlers are a close-knit lot, many of whom have worked together for decades. Each stall is built up around a barrow which is extended at will, as outer and side counters and displays are made up from plastic milk-crates and wooden fruit-boxes. In general the street side of the stall is for selling from and the pavement side for storage; but towards the end of the week the stalls spread halfway across the street, and then you can buy from both front and back. In the late afternoon the decks are cleared, the forecourts dismantled and the roof spars folded away, and the barrows are dragged off to a

nearby yard for the night. As two or three council men sweep the street, old men and women pick over the jettisoned rubbish for anything edible. Then the street empties and is left to the small groups of drinkers who emerge from the bingo exits to continue their parties on the stray barrows left out overnight.

A few minutes' walk away are the leafy terraces and crescents of Camden Town, its doss-house, ex-piano factory, and pubs, and the canal-side villas over the railway in Primrose Hill. On the next two pages are some drawings of them. The Edinburgh Castle with its nice garden was an old haunt of Dylan Thomas; since these drawings were made, someone set light to it with petrol and burnt it down.

Inverness Street market, Camden Town

164

Inverness Street market

Canal near Gloucester Avenue

Arlington House

Gloucester Crescent

St Mark's Crescent

Regent's Park Terrace

The Edinburgh Castle garden

Chalcot Crescent, Primrose Hill

Gloucester Crescent, Camden Town

Ladbroke Grove and Notting Hill

Notting Hill has two faces, one sedate and white, one uproarious and black. The sedate bit centres on the fine stucco crescents and terraces of the Ladbroke Estate, separated by big well-wooded communal gardens, which circle the top of the hill. Architecturally the high-water mark is Stanley Gardens, whose two terraces are tall and densely packed but whose pillared porticos and richly applied decoration skilfully subdue the barrack-like effect. A handsome Italianate church rises at the far end. It all looks spectacular as long as the shiny stucco is kept in good repair and well-painted.

But this kind of elegance is expensive to maintain. Down the road in Ladbroke Grove, with far less money about, the buildings have gone to seed. The railway and Westway cut through at second-floor level and the houses have decayed, even if the process has been arrested at various stages; some are still gracious, some are falling apart, some are merely brick-and-concrete shells. On the other hand, there is a lot going on. The surprising thing about the August Bank Holiday Carnival, apart from the profusion of policemen, the ear-splitting din, the energy and the glitter of the musicians, is the absolute finality with which one kind of London has overtaken another.

Notting Hill Carnival

Stanley Gardens and St Peters Church

Chelsea and the King's Road

Until 1830, the King's Road used to be just what it sounds like: a private road for the King's use on his way to Hampton Court or Kew. Since then it has been the main road through Chelsea, a region first bohemian, then arty, then trendy, then swinging, then *passé* and now a bit of each, every phase having left its own traces; many of the trendiest sixties shops are now closed and branches of the bigger names from the West End established instead. The streets and squares that open off the King's Road are of great variety, some of Olympian grandeur, some done up with candy-coloured Mediterranean fervour. The grandest of all, Royal Avenue, was originally meant to connect Chelsea Hospital with Kensington Palace, but it pegged out at the King's Road. Every May the Flower Show is held in the fine Royal Hospital grounds, but you can't see them for the crush and for all the glasshouses, lawnmowers, weedkillers and gnomes.

Chelsea Flower Show

Royal Avenue from the King's Road

Bywater Street

Carlyle Square

Hendon and Kew

The allotments off Hendon Way are separated from the pavement by wire netting with long grass and blackberries growing through it. Plastic sweet wrappers, old dried dogshit and crushed beer-cans lie at the base. Just behind, an endless stream of loud fast traffic whistles past on the six-lane carriageway. In early September there is a fine crop of tomatoes under the glass; a few of the plots are overgrown and ill-kempt after the holidays. The people digging or working in the hot autumn sun use their wooden sheds like beach huts, for undressing in, as a store, for having a cup of tea from a thermos. Everything in the foreground looks home-made, ingenious and appropriate. Everything else looks mean and second-rate.

London is currently suffering from a rash of round-topped glazed constructions serving as entrances, gangways, penthouses and the like. None have any of the style, imagination and subtlety of Decimus Burton's lovely Palm House at Kew, being renovated as I write. Inside it, as if by magic, all is one: big plant forms seem powerfully structural and its own metal structure looks rooted and organic, as much so in the heavy columns and tautly arching girders as in the exquisite modelling of railings and stairways and the delicate hatching of the thin glazing-bars. It is warm, damp, smells good and contains every known variety of palm.

Allotments by Hendon Way near Brent Cross

The gallery of the Palm House, Kew Gardens

Banana plantains in the Palm House

173

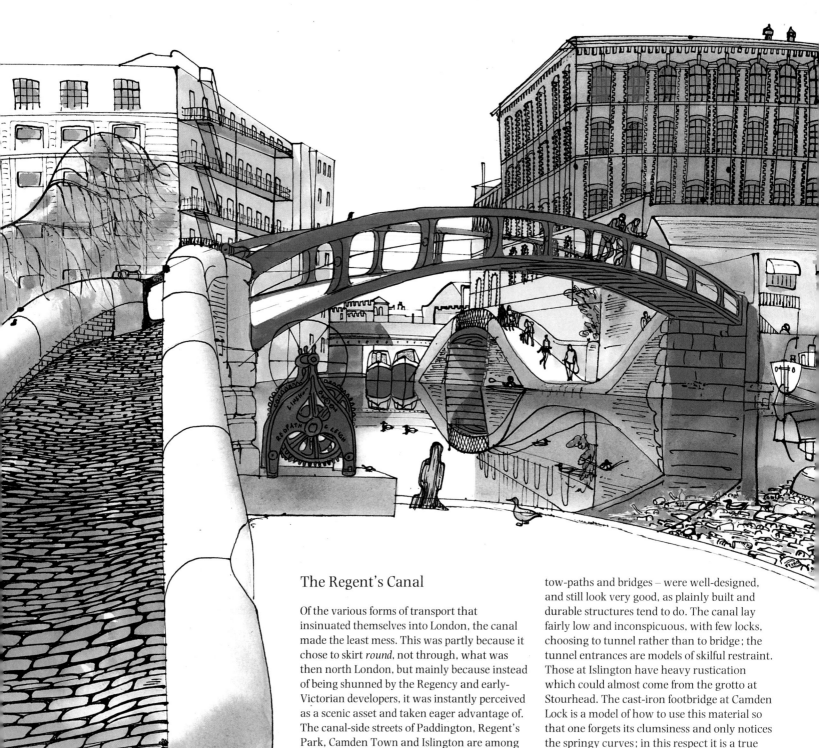

Camden Lock

The Regent's Canal

Of the various forms of transport that insinuated themselves into London, the canal made the least mess. This was partly because it chose to skirt *round*, not through, what was then north London, but mainly because instead of being shunned by the Regency and early-Victorian developers, it was instantly perceived as a scenic asset and taken eager advantage of. The canal-side streets of Paddington, Regent's Park, Camden Town and Islington are among the prettiest developments of the nineteenth century; Blomfield Road in Maida Vale and the hanging gardens of Islington between Noel Road and Vincent Terrace remind one of how little it needs to make a place beautiful. But the canal itself, however useful, never made much money and by the economic criteria admired today it should have been abandoned and filled in long ago.

Nash knew he was creating a new landscape, though this was incidental, never an end in itself. But under his guidance, the practical necessities of the canal – warehousing, locks,

tow-paths and bridges – were well-designed, and still look very good, as plainly built and durable structures tend to do. The canal lay fairly low and inconspicuous, with few locks, choosing to tunnel rather than to bridge; the tunnel entrances are models of skilful restraint. Those at Islington have heavy rustication which could almost come from the grotto at Stourhead. The cast-iron footbridge at Camden Lock is a model of how to use this material so that one forgets its clumsiness and only notices the springy curves; in this respect it is a true descendent of the Iron Bridge itself. The iron, and the stone parapets nearby, are deeply scored with the marks of the bargees' hawsers. There are fine nineteenth-century warehouses at Camden Lock, and behind King's Cross near Battlebridge Basin. Unwanted but protected buildings like these burn down with surprising frequency, only to be replaced by useful but dull ones run up for a shorter life. In 1937 Gilbey's, and Camden Town, were lucky to get from Chermayeff a canal-side building both new and stylish, whose white concrete accords perfectly with the industrial scene around it.

The canal between Noel Road and Vincent Terrace

Tunnel entrance, Islington

Blomfield Road and Maida Avenue

The canal behind St Pancras

The stretch of canal through Pathfield behind St Pancras and King's Cross stations gives surprising interest to a wasteland whose desolation was entirely the work of a second and much more disruptive form of transport, the railways. They covered the surrounding districts in soot, smoke and din, only dispersed 140 years later by diesel and electrification; they endowed them with a long-term legacy of goods-yards and mean housing built for their own poorly paid employees; and they isolated them, since the north–south railway lines themselves formed unbridgeable barriers to east–west movement.

The Regent's Canal was still quite new when the railways were built. It affected them markedly for it barred their way, and they had to get over – or under – the difficulty as best they could. If you stand at the end of the King's Cross platforms you can see right through the tunnel as it dips sharply under the canal before emerging into the light beyond it; whereas at St Pancras the platforms were raised a storey above street level to allow the lines to cross over the canal. The gasworks is much older, dating from 1822; the oldest gasholder remaining, of 1861, is still a striking King's Cross sight today.

The most recent element in the scene, the breaker's yard for old caravans, was also the most short-lived. Since this drawing was made, the far bank has been cleared up and imaginatively restored as a protected area of inner-city wetland wilderness, with facilities for newts, frogs and tadpoles, herons and ducks. But the old cars piled beyond it, and the equally elegant Post Office Tower, remain.

The railways have their champions and their enthusiasts, but despite its beauty the canal is not much visited by admirers. It is however made good use of by anglers, by canoeing clubs, by joggers and strollers and by the sun-tanned jobless who can drink and sleep on the tow-path undisturbed.

The Regent's Canal and the Camley Street gasholders

Entrance to Chalk Farm tunnel

ILL RD K CHAMBERS

O LONGS TRAVEL

Station on the old Hampstead line

The railways and the underground

To begin with, the railways put on the best face they could afford to. They employed grandiloquent rhetoric not just for the stations but for the engineering too. Nowadays alterations are cheaper-looking, but even in the early days everything looked best from the front: the back views, like that onto the entrance to Chalk Farm tunnel from Primrose Hill Road, are like window-displays or stage-sets seen from the wrong side. North-central London being hilly, the railways tunnelled quite frequently; but south of the river, having to raise themselves enough to cross the Thames, they were built more often at first-floor or viaduct level, or even, as at Brixton, criss-crossing over each other higher still. Whole south London communities grew up under the shadow of the railway lines, beginning the process whereby the middle classes moved out of central London: only the richest and the poorest stayed put. The process was continued and extended by the underground but at first steam-powered Metropolitan and District railways and later by the electrified underground proper, which through City caution was originally American-financed. The red-tiled and grandly arched stations of the Hampstead line (now the Northern) mark the last of the private-sector ventures. The whole system combined in 1933 into London Transport, which under Frank Pick became a pioneer in engineering, design and architecture and developed a true corporate identity long before the term had even been invented.

STATION ROAD

Brixton Station on the Southern Region

Eversleigh Road, Battersea: the Shaftesbury Park Estate

Hammersmith Grove

Terraces and semis

The most noticeable thing about Victorian terraced housing for the working and middle classes was not the mean scale or even the low-budget building restrictions: it was simply the endless repetition of the same units, front porch, parlour with bay window, two bedroom windows upstairs, low-pitched Welsh slate roof, shared chimney-stack and kitchen projection at the back, all repeated house after house, street after street, suburb after suburb. The long suburban terraces spawned by the railways were by no means all uniformly dreary. Often they were very prettily detailed and, being only two-storeyed, they let plenty of sunlight into the streets. But repetitive they certainly were – even such good tries as the leafy and philanthropic Shaftesbury Park cottages in

Battersea, with 1135 dwellings more or less continuously arranged, could not fail to be. So a reaction set in, at first consisting simply of the familiar terrace units, as repetitive as ever but now slightly separated; there are pleasant examples in Hammersmith Grove. Norman Shaw's Bedford Park, Chiswick, *c.* 1880, was a more radical reaction against uniformity, a bit more bohemian, and very influential. Shaw's eclecticism – Dutch gables, English brickwork and Norman arches – created an elastic idiom which worked well in this quiet garden suburb, well-wooded and off the main road. It also established the semi as the norm for the long post-1918 years of ribbon development along the new arterial roads; but these proved in the long run to be a much more hostile environment. Architectural scholarship (never much use on its own) was out, easily-tacked-on

Tudor-type timbers and tile-hanging were in, the houses did their very best to look individual and they had nice big front gardens down onto pavements planted with flowering trees. It was a practical and appealing formula, seen at its best along Hendon Way but widely repeated elsewhere. The drawback was that soon the roads, unable to take the ever-heavier and faster traffic, got brutally widened, occasionally with comic but dire results, as at the Vale. The grass verges turned into oil-stained car-stands; ugly barriers, tunnels and bridges had to be built so you could reach your opposite neighbours in one piece. Nevertheless, the suburban semi-detached house remained such an esteemed form that where, to save money, houses had to be built in terraces, they now did their best to look not like terraces at all, but genuine 1920s mock-Tudor semis.

Woodstock Road, Bedford Park, Chiswick

Hendon Way

Cricklewood Lane

The Vale, Cricklewood

North Circular Road at Neasden

Tollgate, College Road, Dulwich

Hendon Way from Cricklewood Lane

Westway near Latimer Road

Turnpikes and motorways

The third and most disruptive intrusion borne by London was the car's. But to begin with, London's roads luckily proved quite adaptable. Only one or two had remained more or less unchanged for a couple of centuries, like the toll road at Dulwich, though this now has a very self-conscious look to it. So most early motorists leaving London still had to make do either with the main roads left by the Romans (Watling Street, Edgware Road, Ermine Street, Bishopsgate and so on) or with the eighteenth-century turnpikes like Tottenham Court Road

and Mile End Road. Only in the 1930s were proper motor roads like Hendon Way, the North Circular, Eastern Avenue, the Great West Road and Western Avenue laid out, with space for strips of houses or light industry on either side. These roads were quite generously conceived, with trees and grassy verges; but road-widening and the sheer weight of traffic have made them dismal places now except for occasional blossomy moments of springtime glory. Motorways however have created an entirely new landscape, or rather two. One is a brisk, efficient and optimistic world of rooftops and blue roadsigns offering instant escape with

nothing to pay. The other, which most drivers never see, lies underneath: a desolate and shadowy wasteland of streaked concrete and well-nigh unusable waste space, tarted up with unlooked-at murals and 'leisure' enclosures and fringed appropriately with car-breakers' yards. There is a classic example of the genre near Latimer Road, where the M41 joins Westway. Abandoned and pillaged cars lie about beneath the motorway because it is worth no one's while to cart them off to the breaker's. This is a sight to bear in mind while glancing at the car ads; this is how they finally park, piled and clinging like mating toads.

Freston Road, North Kensington

Neasden terraces from the North Circular Road

View of Paddington from Westway

Neasden, Paddington and Brixton

Many people never see suburbia except through a car-window; it is too big to take in any other way. It is laborious even to try: the North Circular, for example, is not meant for walking along, the cat-walks and grassy bits and the considerately provided footbridges only adding to the mileage. But it is worth it for the vision of London offered. The sea of tiles at Neasden is one way of housing Londoners, the North Kensington and Westbourne Park high-rise flats another; both have their detractors and their champions, and move in and out of professional favour much as hem-lines move up

and down. But there is one significant difference between them. The Neasden type of houses are rather more likely to have been built on virgin fields, the high-rises more probably on a site where quite good houses have been demolished. The imminent prospect of such demolition naturally causes the particular kind of decay known as planning blight, which is irreversible: after it has set in no one really much minds when the houses are finally pulled down except the people who live in them. A lot of London has vanished like this since the 1950s only to be replaced by new housing dearer, nastier and less durable. By now, London knows more about the costs of

maintaining cheap and shoddy new building and probably will not make the mistake twice; but of course the damage has been done. Indeed the destruction has been on such a scale that, visiting Brixton just after its notorious riots, it was hard to distinguish between riot damage and the general devastation caused by decay, blight and redevelopment.

One alternative is to put the thought of *people* out of one's mind altogether and build flyovers above them. The pedestrian's view of the River Brent at Brent Cross, on the next two pages, shows what happens, with the Brent beginning to go the way of the Fleet, and the people slung as if on a rope ladder.

Chaucer Road from Railton Road, Brixton

The River Brent at Brent Cross

The Thames and Glovers Island from Richmond Hill

The Thames at Richmond

Standing on Richmond Hill and looking down over Petersham Meadows, Glovers Island and Marble Hill Park, one can still occasionally imagine how it must have felt when all London was at one's back and the real country stretched out in front; when Ham House and Marble Hill House were not yet enclosed in suburbia but were outposts of elegance in a landscape of villages and flooding water-meadows, ferries and fish-weirs. But what really matters about suburban London, as about the city as a whole, is the way it is now and the way it will go on developing.

At the right time of year, and in a good light, one can glimpse this easily enough. The view is sharp and informative: pockets of parkland, tall white flats, bits of light industry and wooded suburbia and trading estates stretching away to the big Heathrow hangars where the airliners surge upwards or gently sink. On such occasions one can see enough to realize that, wherever its boundary happens currently to be defined, London is really still – as always – just spreading on and on. Checked here, thrusting there, it goes on gradually but relentlessly absorbing and transforming places whose original separate identities are not blotted out overnight but instead grow bit by bit less distinct. In the end, even if their names remain, the original associations vanish. Few people now know or remember that those familiar London names Tyburn, Holborn, Westbourne and Fleet used once to signify not bricks and mortar, concrete and asphalt, but water: clear streams which – like the Thames itself – could be seen winding between the fields and gleaming or rippling in the light breezes.

Author's note

I am indebted to the following works for the light they shed on the historical and architectural aspects of London:

The Buildings of England: London by Nikolaus Pevsner (Penguin, 2 vols, 1952 and 1973)

Georgian London by John Summerson (Penguin, 1978)

A Guide to the Architecture of London by Edward Jones and Christopher Woodward (Weidenfeld, 1983)

The London Encyclopaedia, edited by Ben Weinreb and Christopher Hibbert (Macmillan, 1983)

I would like also to thank those who have allowed me to draw them or to make drawings of or from their buildings.

I am particularly grateful to John Curtis and his colleagues at Weidenfeld and Nicolson, and also to Sally Mapstone, for their help and encouragement throughout.

Index

Figures in *italics* refer to illustrations.

Adam, Robert, *130, 157*
Admiralty Arch, 78
Albany Barracks, 103
Albert Bridge, *31*
Albert Buildings, Queen Victoria Street, *48*
Albert Court, *150, 151*
Albert Embankment, 28
Albert Hall, *150, 151*
Albert Hall Mansions, *150, 151*
Albert Memorial, Kensington Gardens, *98, 99*, 150
All Souls, Langham Place, *136, 137*
Alton East Estate, 50
Angel, Islington, *162*
Anne, Queen of Great Britain, 98
Anne (of Denmark), Queen of James I, *17*
Apsley House, *10*, 144, *144–5*
Archer, Thomas, 72
Arlington House, Camden Town, 166
Athenaeum (club), *86, 87*
Austin Friars, 53

Baker, Herbert, 35, 48
Bank of England, 35, 48, *49*
Bankside Power Station, *22, 22*
Banqueting Hall, Whitehall, *11*, 69, 76
Barbican, *10, 11*, 26, 34, 50, *51*
Barnes Bridge, *31*
Barry, Sir Charles, 28, 86
Barry, Edward, 126
Battersea, 30
  Power Station, *30, 30*
  vegetable-growing, 152
  houses, *180, 180*
Battlebridge Basin, Regent's Canal, *174*
Bayswater, 98
Bazalgette, Sir Joseph, 31
Bedford estate, 121
Bedford family, 8
Bedford Park, Chiswick, *180, 181*
Bedford Square, 8, 88, 89, 115
Bedford, Francis Russell, 4th Earl of, *128*
Belgrave Square, 88, 89, 148
Belgravia, 8, 20, 115, 140, 148, 163
Berkeley Square, 115, 138, *138–9*
Bermondsey, 19, 20, *20*, 24
Berry Brothers & Rudd's, St James's Street, 82, *82*
Big Ben, 28, 68, 69
Billingsgate, 36, 42
Birdcage Walk, 92
Bishopsgate, 50, 53, 183
Blackfriars, *12, 22*
Blackfriars Bridge, 9, 22, *22*, 49
Blackheath, 37, 154, *155*
Blake, William, 61, *111*
Bleeding Heart Yard, Holborn, 54
Blomfield Road, Maida Vale, *174, 175*
Bloomsbury, 115, 121
Boodle's (club), 82
Boswell, James, 45
Boulton & Watt, 150
Brent (river), 153, 185, *186–7*
Brent Cross, 153, 172, 185, *186–7*
Brick Lane, *63, 63*
  market, 65
British Broadcasting Corporation, *136, 137*
British Museum (and Library), *120, 121*
Brixton, 185, *185*
  Railway Station, 178, *179*
Brompton Road, 146, *147*

Brook Gate: view from, *143*
Brook Street, 140
Brooks's (club), 82
Broomfield Hill, Richmond Park: view from, *113*
Buckingham Palace, 8, 69, 74, 80, *80*
  gardens, 144
Bunhill Fields, 9, 61, *61*
Bunyan, John, 61
Burton, Decimus, 86, 144, *144–5*, 172
Bywater Street, Chelsea, *171*

Cambria (Thames barge), 20, *20*
Cambridge Circus (near), 116
Camden High Street, 162
Camden Lock, *137, 137*, 164, *164, 174, 174*
Camden Town, 9, 164, 166, 167, 174
Camley Street gas-holders, *176–7*
Cannon Street Station and bridge, *10, 23, 23*
Carlton Gardens, *86, 87*
Carlton House, 86, 115
Carlyle Square, Chelsea, *171*
Carnaby Street, 115
Caroline Terrace, Belgravia, *163*
Carter Lane (City), 52, *54*
Cavendish family, 8
Cenotaph, Whitehall, 69
Centre Point, *37, 98, 130*
Chalcot Crescent, Primrose Hill, *166*
Chalk Farm, 9, *104, 178, 179*
Charles I, King: statue, 84
Charles II, King, 45, 78, 92
Chaucer Road, Brixton, *184*
Chelsea, 170, *170–1*
  pottery, 152
  Flower Show, *170, 170*
Chelsea Bridge, *31*
Chermayeff, Serge, 174
Chiswick, *32–3, 32*
  Eyot, *32*
  Norman Shaw houses, 180
Chiswick House, *156, 157*
Christ Church, Newgate Street, *44, 44–5*
Christ Church, Spitalfields, *62, 62*
Church Row, Hampstead, 152, *160, 160*
City of London, 8
  post-Fire rebuilding, 8, 35, 48
  Wren churches, 8, 9, 24, 35, 36, *44–5, 52*
  boundaries, 9
  views *26–7*, 36, 37, 60
  described, 35, *45–6*, 48
  ceremonial, *46, 46*
  post-war building, 50–2, 60
City of London Club, 52, *53*
Clapham, 152
Claypit Hill, Epping Forest, *112*
Clement's Lane, 52, *52*
Coach and Horses (pub), Hill Street, *122*
Coade stone, 52
Coade Stone Works, 28
Coal Exchange, 52
Coliseum theatre, *124, 124*
Columbia Road, 67
  market, *64, 65*
Commercial Road, 68
Commercial Union building (City), 35, *47*
Commons, House of, *70–1, 70*; *see also* Parliament
Conduit Street, 140
Connaught Hotel, 140
Conran, Sir Terence, 130
Constable, John, 152
Constitution Hill, 144
Cork Street, 115
Cornelissen (shop), Great Queen Street, 146, *147*
Cornhill, 42
County Hall, 9, *13, 28, 28–9*

Courage's brewery, 20
Covent Garden, 8
  piazza, *11, 88, 89, 128, 128–9*
  former appearance, *62*
  boutiques, 115
  Ellen Keeley in, *116*
  see also Royal Opera House
Cricklewood Lane, *181*; view from, *182*
Cross Keys (pub), Endell Street, *122, 123*
Crystal Palace
  mast, 36
  dinosaurs, *111, 111*
Cubitt, Lewis, *134, 148*
Cumberland Terrace, Regent's Park, *100, 101*
Curlew Street, 20

Daily Mirror building, Holborn, 54, *54–5*
Dance, George, 46, 110
Davies Street, 140, *140*
Dean Street, Soho, *118*
Dean's Yard, Westminster, *10*, 69, *72, 72*
Defence, Ministry of (Whitehall), 69, 76, *77*
Defoe, Daniel, 61
Deptford, *13*
Deutsche Bank building, Bishopsgate, 35, *50, 50*
Dickens Inn, St Katharine's Dock, *11*
Dickens, Charles, 54
Discovery (ship), 20
District railway, 179
docks, 18, 66
Downing Street, 69, 80, *81*
Downshire Hill, Hampstead, 160, *161*
D'Oyly Carte company, 124
Duke of York's column and steps, Waterloo Place, *86, 86*
Duke Street, Mayfair, 140
  piazza off, *140*
Dulwich, 152, 154, *154*
  toll, *182, 183*

East End, 10, 35, 65–6
Eastcheap, 35
Eastern Avenue, 183
Eaton Square, 148
Eccleston Mews, *149*
Economist building, St James's, 82
Edgware Road, 183
Edinburgh Castle (pub), Camden Town, *164, 166*
Embankment Gardens, Westminster, 69, 76, *76*
Embankment Place, *77*
Epping Forest, 91, *112, 112*
Ermine Street, 183
Euston Road, 115, *132–3, 133–4*
Euston Station, *134, 135*
Evelyn, John, 8
Eversleigh Road, Battersea, *180*

Farringdon Road, *65, 65*
Felixstowe, 66
Fenchurch Street, 42
Fenton House, Hampstead, 152, *157, 157*
Festival of Britain (1951), 9
'fifty new churches' Act (1711), 68
Finch, Lady Isabella, 138
Finsbury Circus, 35
Finsbury Fields, 61
Fire of London, Great (1666), 8, 35
Fitzrovia, 115, 130
Fitzroy Square, *130, 131*
Flanagan, Barry, *59, 59*
Fleet (river), 185, 189
Fleet Street, 52, 54
Floral Hall, Covent Garden, *126, 126*
Foreign Office, 8, 69, 92
Foster, Norman, 137

Fournier Street (Spitalfields), 48, *48, 62, 63*
Fowler, Charles, 128
French, The (Soho pub), 118
Friary Court, St James's Palace, 82, *82*
Fribourg & Treyer (shop), Haymarket, 146, *147*
Fulham, 158
Fulham Road, *147*
Furnival's Inn, Holborn, 54

George II, King: statue, 118
George IV, King (*formerly* Prince Regent), 101, 115
Gerrard Street, *118, 118*
Gibbons, Grinling, 84
Gibbs, James, 85
Gibson Square, Islington, 163
Gilbey's building, Camden Town, *174*
Gill, Eric, *137*
Gloucester Avenue, Camden Town: canal near, *166*
Gloucester Crescent, Camden Town, *166–7*
Glovers Island, *188–9, 189*
Golden Square, Soho, *118, 118*
Gordon, Gen. Charles George, 69
Gough Square, 54
Gower Street, 121
Great Queen Street, 146, *147*
Great West Road, 183
Greek Street, *119*
Green Park, 91, 94, 95, 96
Greenwich, 9, 13, 16, 17, 91, 152, 154, *155*
Grocers' Hall, 48
Grosvenor Chapel, South Audley Street, 140, *140*
Grosvenor Crescent, *148, 148*
Grosvenor Square, 140, *141*
Grosvenor family, 8
Grosvenor, Sir Richard, 140
Guards Memorial, Horse Guards, *74–5*
Guildhall, 35, *47, 47*
Guy's Hospital, 36

Hackney Road, Haggerston, *163*
Ham Gate, Richmond Park, *112*
Ham House, 152, *156, 157, 188*
Hammersmith, 13, *31*
  Mall, 31
Hammersmith Bridge, *31, 31*
Hammersmith Grove, 180, *180*
Hampstead, 152, 157–8, 160, *160–1*
  Tube station, 179
Hampstead Heath, 91, 106, 107, *108–9*
  Ponds, *106, 107*
Hampstead Heath Road, *160, 163*
Hardwick, Philip, 134
Harrods store, Brompton Road, 146, *147*
Haverstock Hill, Hampstead, 158
Hawksmoor, Nicholas, 17, 35, 62, 72, 98
Haymarket, *124, 125, 147*
Heal's store, Tottenham Court Road, 130
Hendon Way, *172, 172*, 180, *181, 182, 183*
Henrietta Street, 128
Henry VIII, King, 13, 74, 82, 92
Hertford Canal, 110
Hilton Hotel, Park Lane, 98
Hogarth Roundabout, Chiswick, *32*
Hogarth, William, 59
Holborn, 54, 55
  river, 189
Home Office, *78, 78*
Horse Guards, 9, 69, *74–5, 75*, 92
  Parade, 74
Horse Guards Avenue, *77*
Huguenots, 63, 152
Hungerford Bridge, 26, 69, 76, *77*
Hurlingham Club and House, *158, 158*

Hyde Park, 91, 96, *96, 97, 98, 98, 142, 143*
Hyde Park Corner, 144, *144–5*

Imperial Institute, 150
Inn on the Park, 98
Inns of Court, 10
Inverness Street market, *164, 164–5*
Ironmongers' Almshouses, Kingsland Road, 49
Isle of Dogs, 37
Islington, 9, 152, *162, 163*, 174, *175*
  Tunnel, *175*

Jama Masjid, Spitalfields, 62
James I, King, 92
Jermyn Street, 146, *147*
Johnson, Samuel, 54
Jones, Sir Horace, 42
Jones, Inigo
  Covent Garden piazza, 8, 88, 128
  Banqueting Hall, *11*, 69, 76
  Queen's House, Greenwich, *17*
  Lindsey House, Lincoln's Inn Fields, *59, 59*
  chapel, St James's, 82
  town planning, 115

Keats Grove, Hampstead, 9, *160*
Keats, John, 106, 160
Keeley, Ellen, 116
Kensington Gardens, 91, 96, 98, *98, 99*
Kensington Palace, 98, 99
Kent, William, 9, 69, 74, 138
Kenwood House, 9, 106, *107, 108–9, 157, 157*
Kew: Palm House, *172, 173*
King Street (City), 8
King Street (Covent Garden), 128
King William Street (City), 37
King's Cross Station, *134, 135, 174, 176*
King's Reach, *13*, 26, *26–7*
King's Road, Chelsea, 149, 170, *171*
Kingsway, Holborn, 115
Knightsbridge Barracks, 96, 98, *98*

LBC studios, Gough Square, 54
Ladbroke Grove, *168, 168*
Lamb and Flag (pub), Rose Street, *122*
Landseer, Sir Edwin, 84
Langham Hotel, *137*
Langham Place, *136, 137*
Lasdun, Sir Denys, 26
Latimer Road, North Kensington: near, *183, 183*
Law Courts, Strand, 57, *58*
  appeal court in session, *57*
Lawrence, T. N. & Sons, 54
Leadenhall Market, *42, 42*
Leadenhall Street, 24, 35
Leicester Square, 10
Leverton, Thomas, 8
Libyan People's Bureau, St James's Square, 88
Limehouse Basin, 66, *67*
Limehouse Cut, 67
Lincoln's Inn, 10
Lincoln's Inn Fields, 57, *59, 59*, 152
Lindsey House, Lincoln's Inn Fields, *59, 59*
Lisle Street, *118, 118*
Liverpool Street Station, 49, 53
Lloyds (City), 35, 36
Lock, James & Co. Ltd (shop), St James's Street, 82
London Bridge, 24, 35, 36, 110
London Transport, 178
London Wall, 7, 35, *39, 39*, 50, *50, 52*
Long Water, Kensington Gardens, *98, 99*
Lord North Street, *72, 73*

Lords, House of, 70; see also Parliament
Lower Thames Street, 36
Ludgate Hill, 53
Ludgate Square, 52, 52
Lutyens, Sir Edwin, 35, 142

M4 (road), 32, 153
M41 (road), 183
Macclesfield Bridge ('Blow-up'), Regent's Canal, 102, 103
Maida Avenue, 175
Maida Vale, 174
Mall, The, 78, 78, 95
Mansion House, 35, 46, 53
Mansion House Square, 52, 53
Mappin & Webb, Mansion House Square, 52, 53
Marble Arch, 143
Marble Hill Park (and House), Richmond, 189
markets, 65, 65; see also individual markets
Marlborough House, 82
Mary, Queen of Great Britain, 69, 76
Marylebone Road, 115
Marylebone Station, 134, 135
Mason's Avenue, 53
Mayfair, 140
Mayhew, Henry, 116
Mercers' Hall, 48
Metropolitan railway, 179
Michelin building, Fulham Road, 147
Middle Temple, 57
Middle Temple Lane, 57
Mile End Road, 183
Monument, The (City), 45, 45
Moore, Henry, 99
Moorfields, 61, 152
Mornington Crescent (near), 162
Mortlake: brewery, 32, 33
motorways, 183
Mount Street, 140, 140, 141

Nash, John
  triumphal route, 86
  Regent's Park, 86, 90, 91, 95, 100–3, 115
  Regent's Canal, 92
  terraces, 98, 101
  social engineering, 115
  Theatre Royal, 124
  Regent Street, 137
  and picturesque, 154
  design, 174
National Gallery, 84–5, 85
National Provincial building (City), 52, 53
National Theatre, 9, 26, 26–7
Natural History Museum, 8, 150, 150
NatWest building (and Tower) (City), 10, 11, 25, 26, 35, 36, 50, 51, 52
Neal's Yard (Covent Garden), 126, 126
Neasden, 181, 184, 185
Nelson's column, 84
New Bond Street, 147
New Cross, 152
New Oxford Street, 115, 121, 147
New Road, 134
New Square, Lincoln's Inn, 57, 57
Newton, William, 59
Noel Road, Islington, 174, 175
Nonconformism, 61, 62
North Circular Road, 181, 183, 184, 185
North Kensington, 183, 185
Notting Hill carnival, 168, 169

'Old Bess' pumping-engine, Science Museum, 150, 150
Old Compton Street, 118
Old Deer Park see Richmond Park
Old Ford, 110, 110

Orangery, Kensington Palace, 98, 99
Orpington, 152
Oxford Circus, 115–16
Oxford Street, 115, 146, 147

Paddington, 152, 174, 185
Paddington Station, 134
Palace Theatre, Cambridge Circus, 124, 125
Pall Mall, 86, 87
Palmerston, 3rd Viscount, 8
Park Lane, 10, 95, 142, 143
Parliament, Houses of, 13, 28, 28–9, 71; see also Commons, House of; Lords, House of; Westminster, Palace of
Parliament Hill, 106, 106
Parliament Square, 69, 71
Parson's Green, 158
Pathfield, 176
Paxton & Whitfield (shop), Jermyn Street, 146, 147
Peabody, George, 53
Peckham Rye Common, 111, 111
Pegg's eel stall (near Cambridge Circus), 116
Pembroke, Earls of: effigies, 39
Pennethorne, James, 110
Pentonville Road, Islington, 153, 160, 162
Peter Jones (shop), Sloane Square, 148, 149
Petersham Meadows, Richmond, 189
Petticoat Lane, 65, 65
Piccadilly, 114, 115
Piccadilly Circus, 10, 115
Pickford's Wharf, 24, 24–5
Pilgrim Street (City), 52, 52
Plague, Great (1665), 61
Plough Road, Wandsworth, 152–3
Pond Cottages, Dulwich, 154, 154
Port of London Authority, 37
Portland Place, 137, 140
Post Office Tower (Telecom Tower), 37, 98, 121, 176
Poultry (City), 35
Powell, Sir Philip and Moya, Hidalgo, 50
Preston Road, North Kensington (off), 183
Primrose Hill, 11, 91, 95, 104, 104–5, 164, 166
Primrose Hill Road, 179
Prince of Wales Road, Blackheath, 154, 155
Prudential building, Holborn, 35, 54, 54–5
Pugin, Augustus Welby, 28, 70
Putney, 158
Putney Hill, 159

Quadrant, Regent Street, 137
Queen Anne's Gate, 10, 69, 78, 78–9, 160
Queen Mary's Garden, Regent's Park, 90, 101
Queen Street (City), 8
Queen Victoria Memorial (Mall), 78, 91
Queen Victoria Street (City), 35, 48
Queenhythe, 39, 39

Railton Road, Brixton: view from, 185
railways, 8, 176, 178
Red Lion (pub), Duke of York Street, 122, 122, 123
Reform Club, Pall Mall, 86, 87
Regent Street, 115, 136
Regent's Canal, 101, 103, 103, 110, 174, 175, 176, 176–7
Regent's Canal Dock, 66, 67
Regent's Park
  and Nash scheme, 86, 90, 91, 95, 101, 100–3, 115
  terraces, 98, 101
  and canal, 174
Regent's Park Terrace, 166

Richmond, 189
Richmond Hill, 188, 188–9
Richmond Palace, 112
Richmond Park (Old Deer Park), 91, 112, 113
Rising Sun (pub), Tottenham Court Road, 122, 123
roads, 183–5, 186–7
Robin (ship), 20, 20
Rogers, Richard, 35
Rohe, Mies van der, 50, 52
Ronan Point, 10
Rotherhithe Street (off), 66
Rotten Row, Hyde Park, 96, 96, 98, 99
Round Pond, Kensington Gardens, 98
Royal Avenue, Chelsea, 170, 170–1
Royal Exchange, 35, 47
  fountain near, 52
Royal Free Hospital, Hampstead, 106, 107
Royal Hospital, Chelsea, 170
Royal Naval College, Greenwich, 9, 16–17, 17
Royal Opera Arcade, 86, 86
Royal Opera House, Covent Garden, 85, 126, 126
Ruislip, 152

Saarinen, Eero, 140
St Albans, Henry Jermyn, 1st Earl of, 8
St Andrew's church, Holborn, 52, 53
St Anne's church, Soho, 118, 119
St Benet's church, Paul's Wharf, 24, 52, 52
St Botolph's church, Bishopsgate, 52, 53
St Bride's church, 10, 34, 52, 52
St Edmund the King church, 52
St George's Gardens, Mayfair, 140
St Giles-in-the-Fields church, 130
St James's (district), 8, 69
St James's Hospital, 82, 92
St James's Palace, 9, 69, 82, 82, 83
St James's Park, 10, 78, 86, 91–2, 92–3
St James's Place, 82
St James's Square, 8, 88, 88–9, 123
St James's Street, 82, 82
St John, Chapel of (Tower), 40, 41
St John's church, Smith Square, 72, 73
St John's Chapel, Downshire Hill, 161
St Katharine's Dock, 11, 18, 18, 19, 20, 20, 32, 148
St Mark's Crescent, Camden Town, 166
St Martin's church, Ludgate, 52
St Martin-in-the-Fields church, 85, 124, 124
St Martin's Lane, 124
St Mary Abbots church, Kensington, 99
St Mary-le-Bow (Bow Church), 24, 44, 44–5
St Mary-le-Strand church, 85
St Mary Somerset church, 24
St Nicholas Cole Abbey, 24
St Pancras Station, 134, 134, 176
St Paul's Cathedral
  building, 8, 35, 43, 43, 44–5
  use of space, 9
  views and surrounding contrasts, 10, 22–3, 23, 24, 24–5, 26, 28, 52
  nave, 43
  charnel house, 61
St Paul's church, Covent Garden, 128
St Paul's Walk, 43
St Peter's church, Kensington Park Road, 169

St Stephen's Hall, Palace of Westminster, 70
St Vedast, Foster Lane, 44, 44–5
Salisbury (pub), St Martin's Lane, 122, 123
Science Museum, South Kensington, 150, 150
Scott, Sir George Gilbert, 134
Siefert, Richard, 50, 134
  'Siefert Circus', 130
Selfridges store, Oxford Street, 147
Senate House, University of London, 121, 121
Serpentine, 97
Shad Thames, 10, 13, 20, 20
Shaftesbury Avenue, 115
Shaftesbury Park estate, Battersea, 180, 180
Shaw, Norman, 150, 180
Shell Centre, South Bank, 7, 13, 28
Shoreditch, 152
Sir John Soane's Museum, 9, 59, 59
Skinners' Hall (City), 46, 47
Sloane Square, 148, 149
Smirke, Sir Robert, 121
Smirke, Sydney, 121
Smith Square, 69, 72, 73
Smith, James and Son (shop), New Oxford Street, 146, 147
Smithfield Market, 42, 48
Snowdon aviary, London Zoo, 103, 103
Soane, Sir John, 35, 48, 59; see also Sir John Soane's Museum
Soho, 115, 118–19
Soho Square, 115, 118
Somerset House, 26
Sotheby's, New Bond Street, 146, 147
South Audley Street, 140, 140
South Bank, 9, 13, 24
South Kensington, 150
South Molton Street, 115, 140, 140
Southwark, 24–5, 36
Southwark Bridge, 9
Southwark Cathedral, 24, 24–5, 36
Souvenirs of London (shop), Oxford Street, 147
Speakers' Corner, Hyde Park, 96
Spence, Sir Basil, 98
Spencer House, Green Park, 94, 95
Spitalfields, 9, 48, 62
  market, 62, 64
  silk weaving, 62, 152
Stanley Gardens (Ladbroke Estate), 168, 169
Stepney, 18
Stock Exchange, 35
Strand, 57
street traders, 116, 116
Street, George Edmund, 57
Sun Alliance building, St James's Street, 82, 82
Sun Tavern, Long Acre, 123
Surrey Docks, 13, 66, 66
Sydenham, 36

Taylor Woodrow, 10
Telecom Tower see Post Office Tower
Telford, Thomas, 18
Temple (City), 57
Temple Church, 39, 39
Thames, River, 37
  importance, 9, 13
  bridges, 9
  flood barrier, 10, 13, 14–15
  traffic, 13–14
  at Richmond, 188–9, 189
Thames Street, 13
Theatre Royal, Drury Lane, 124, 125
Theatre Royal, Haymarket, 124, 125
Thompson, J. Walter (advertising agency), 138
Threadneedle Street, 48

Throgmorton Street, 53
Tilbury, 66
Tottenham, 152
Tottenham Court Road, 115, 130, 131, 133, 183
Tower Bridge, 60, 60
Tower Hill, 38, 39, 60
Tower of London, 8–10, 35, 37, 40, 40–1
Trafalgar Square, 69, 84–5, 84–5
Traitor's Gate (Tower), 40, 40
Trajan, Emperor of Rome, 38, 39
'Travellers' Club, Pall Mall, 86, 87
Treasury, 69
Trooping the Colour, 74
turnpike roads, 183
tv-am studios, 11, 137, 137
Tyburn (river), 140, 152, 189

underground railway, 178, 179
United States Embassy, Grosvenor Square, 140, 141
University College, Gower Street, 121
University College Hospital, 121, 121

Vale, The (Cricklewood), 180, 181
Vale of Health, Hampstead Heath, 106
Vanbrugh, Sir John, 17, 98
  Greenwich house (Vanbrugh Castle), 152, 154, 155
Vardy, John, 95
Victoria Embankment, 26, 31
Victoria Park, 91, 110, 110
Victoria Tower (Parliament), 28
Victoria monument see Queen Victoria Memorial
Vincent Terrace, Islington, 174, 175

Wandle (river), 152
Wandsworth, 152, 153, 158
Wapping, 18, 19, 20
Waterhouse, Alfred, 35, 54, 121, 150
Waterloo Bridge, 13, 26
Waterloo Place, 69, 86, 86
Watling Street, 183
Webb, Aston, 150
Webb, John, 17
Wellington Arch, 144
Wembley, 152
West End, 8, 9, 37, 115–16
West India Dock, 67
Westbourne (district), 185
Westbourne (river), 152, 189
Western Avenue, 183
Westminster, 8, 37, 69
Westminster Abbey, 9, 69–72, 72
  Statesmen's Aisle, 70, 71
Westminster Bridge, 9, 13
Westminster, Palace of, 28, 69–70; see also Parliament
Westway, 153, 168, 183, 183, 185
Whitehall, 8, 10, 69
Whitehall Court, 76, 76, 92
Whitehall Palace, 69, 74, 76
White's (club), 82
William III, King, 88, 98
Wilton Crescent, 148, 148
Woodstock Road, Bedford Park, 181
Woolwich Arsenal, 154
Wordsworth, William, 13
Wren, Sir Christopher
  City plan, 8, 35, 45
  City churches, 8, 9, 24, 35, 36, 44–5, 52
  Royal Naval Hospital, 9, 13, 16, 17
  and St Paul's, 43–5
  river steps, 69, 76
  Charles I statue, 84
  on pomp, 101
Wyatt, Benjamin Dean, 124

Yevele, Henry, 71–2

Zoological Gardens, 103, 103